A fascinating, light-hearted and enjoyable ⌐
the disciplines of school education with an en⌐
good general health. A 'Haynes manual' for ⌐
and the soul.

– David Stewart, peace officer

I was incredibly impressed with David's first book and so there was a lot of anticipation for *The Back Doctor's School of Health*. Expectations were high but this book really delivers. David has managed to achieve something very difficult – namely, allowing the layman to understand the intricate complexities of the human body and how, through its connection with the mind, we can have a healthy body and live life the way humans are meant to. If you want to understand how amazing the human body is and how it is relatively straightforward to create good health (without fancy diets, crazy exercises or huge amounts of medication) then this is the book for you. Highly recommended and I am already looking forward to David's next book!

Alberto Giovino, recruitment consultant

I have awaited this second book by David with anticipation. David has a strong commitment to deliver knowledge to people of all ages and this book does just that. He has a fun, playful style of writing which helped me easily digest the subject of good health. David's desire to share his own outlook on health and good living to his clients and community is praiseworthy. He does not hesitate to address those areas he sees as important and by doing so he creates a wave of energy which will only enhance life for those around him.

I have attended David's practice in Haywards Heath for some time and know that he is genuinely dedicated to those in his care, his community and the world at large. David's enthusiasm for our well being is at the heart of all he does.

– Julia King, client

Coming from a fitness and yoga back ground I found David's book *The Back Doctor's School of Health* an extremely interesting and educational read. David's book has opened up my eyes to how truly magnificent the human body is and how much goes on every nanosecond of the day without our conscious minds even knowing. David has written his book in such a style that it is easy to follow, informative, educational without being too medically complicated. *The Back Doctor's School of Health* explains how masterful the dynamic engineering of our bodies are from a microscopic cell to the function of the internal organs and much more. David explains beautifully how we can help look after our amazing bodies; keeping the physical and internal body strong, flexible, mobile and free from dis-ease and disease through exercise, diet and mental attitude.

I love David's honesty and truthfulness when he briefly writes about his own mental health journey; the effects it had on his physical health and how he overcame these traumas through a holistic approach rather than prescribed man-made drugs. This book has helped me understand the crucial working of the internal human mechanism in an easy and understandable manner which I am extremely grateful for. *The Back Doctor's School of Health* will be my go-to book for advice and answers in my continued journey in yoga and holistic healing. I truly hope and prayer that David's vision of a new health system will one day come to light and we can start stepping away from the multi-billion-profit performing pharmaceutical drug companies, but instead start to trust the amazing capability of our magnificent organism the human Body!

– Diana Laker-Fullilove, yoga/fitness teacher & holistic healing therapist

And if you don't believe those people, here's what my own sister has to say about my book...

Enlightening, full of fun facts and an engaging read. *The Back Doctor's School of Health* is a holistic guide broken down into exercise and lifestyle tips detailing the dos and don'ts of preparing to live a healthy life, in an understandable language, which is not bombarded with medical jargon. I learnt tools of how to master mindfulness and manage my emotions. My brother's personality shines through with his wittiness and serenity.

I found the concept of living a principled life deeply profound, we are in control of our destiny, you are what you are because of your beliefs, and I believe we reap what you sow, as our dad used to say when we were younger 'knowledge is power' and David is giving you that power.

– Helen Tennison, sister of author

Reviews for the author's previous book, *The Back Doctor Secrets*:

*****

I found this a very interesting and thought provoking book which gave me an insight into the options I have to take care of myself rather than rely on GPs who just write a prescription with out offering any alternatives.
    – Carol Dodson

*****

A lovely inspiring read. One main lesson which is permeated throughout this book is the concept we should empower ourselves to look within and take control and accountability of our own health, wellbeing and seeker of truth and knowledge. David lays out the tools in this book to enable every individual to do this. Also intrigued to read section on vaccinations and big pharma. He provides a broad insight whilst remaining sensitive to the reader, due to this being such a controversial and triggering topic for many, especially during this time of Covid. I would implore anyone to read with an open mindset as I, myself am aware of how much of a complex minefield it can be, having delved into the history and efficacy of this topic for some years.
    – Helen C.

The Back Doctor's
School of Health

Volume One

Health Essentials

David Tennison

Hybrid Practitioner

Production: www.preparetopublish.com
Cover design: www.wheelhousedesign.co.uk

Contents

For liberty and the great principle
of raising collective knowledge

'It is more important to know what sort of person has a disease
than to know what sort of disease a person has'
– attributed to Hippocrates, first hybrid practitioner
c.460–c.370 BC (a long time ago) .

The search for truth

I am limited to a human form therefore I am flawed,
But by recognising those flaws, I am limitless.
I feel fear and by recognising my fears, I am fearless.
I feel love and by recognising my love I am loved.
Love always overcomes fear in time,
As love is timeless and fear is monetary
Love is a truth and fear is a perception
To feel love or fear is a choice. I see this, do you see the same?

The Living Dream

Now I see, it must be, I must die, without a sigh,
But in my grief, I know life is brief.
I could be hit by a bus, so I must not rush
But I must keep pace, in the tortoise race,
Taking care on life's stair, but the weight I bear,
means wear and tear,
a bell is rung, last orders have come,
my will is done, on Earth as it is in heaven
so rest in peace, forever at least.
On the final flight, into the light;
Looking down to rising tears in falling beers,
at a wake for my sake,
Know I am free, eternal me, let's hope not too long in purgatory
Now I see, it is meant to be.

Foreword

By Tim Rylatt

(Author of *Business Battleships*, *Growing by Design* and *The Missing Business Instructions*)

I was delighted when David asked me to read his latest book. The previous one (*The Back Doctor Secrets*) was great, and I was keen to learn more about the way that we all work as human beings and how our health can be impacted by the decisions we make and the way we choose to think.

I say 'choose to think' as so often in life we are very reactive creatures. The tendency is to react to external stimuli, and for our behaviour to be driven by semi- or even fully automatic responses.

When it comes to our health, however, which is the long-term result of daily decisions and our mindset towards making those decisions, there is a fantastic opportunity to do things better!

That is why this new book from David is so important.

It forces us to carefully consider the way we look at health as a whole and to deeply explore our mindset, belief system, and even our own character.

This is a good thing. It is something that should happen more often in life.

Within my own career history, I have been a student of geology, an operational police officer, a trainer, and a business coach. I currently own three businesses and have a team of staff to engage with and manage, along with the natural stresses, strains and fun that brings. My experience has given me a particular set of skills and a mindset to match, but it has also created a setting where often health management had become a secondary consideration from day to day. This book has helped to highlight that and draw it back into a position of rightful importance in my mind.

What I found particularly interesting within these pages was the level of overlap that David's experience in life and helping others has with my own.

The concept of 'Stoical Beingism' resonated strongly with me, and the explanation he gives of a military mindset and kinship amongst peers certainly stretches into my own experience of working within an emergency service. The approach to developing a healthy mindset recommended, and the process for doing so, were new to me, and genuinely helpful too.

Reading this book has been extremely interesting and has reminded me that where much of my own life is highly systematic, organised, and driven by numbers, it is also important to stop and take time to breathe, relax, and focus on health and wellbeing too.

I suspect that many people who pick this book up will be looking for what I was at the time; some inspiration, some fresh ideas, and a little bit of professional challenge to some unhealthy embedded attitudes and behaviours.

If you are seeking a resource that offers fascinating concepts, pragmatic ideas, and a new means of thinking about health (and many other things) I can highly recommend reading on...

Preface

If you read my first book, *The Back Doctor Secrets*, then you will know I am an accidental author. In 2020 I was called to act in reaction to the UK government's approach to a 'flu-like' virus of short duration that was being falsely reported as ten times deadlier than in reality. I was filled with sadness at a premonition of a new dark age, so in protest I decided to put my energy into a cause I believed in, which produced a book. During the writing and editing phase I felt strong and purposeful but when I finished the book the sadness returned; the world was still the way it was and is.

I realized my work wasn't done. That my life must be dedicated to helping people raise their knowledge on health matters so that we are no longer fooled by systems designed to take the power away from the people. The game is rigged and not in your favour as the individual and the people.

Some individuals and people are benefiting from these systems which encourage self-seeking behaviour, but ultimately in the end we all lose if our loved ones die prematurely because they can't access healthcare or because people are left to become sick unnecessarily, in the interests of suiting a certain business model which takes no burden of responsibility and is not held to account, for what in my eyes are criminal acts. I knew then I had to continue to write.

I wanted to write a book simplifying the subject of health; however I first had to understand how complex and diverse that subject is. My continuous study of health has meant I've spent large chunks of time reading textbooks and journals, in order to distil my learning into this book, as my version of the need-to-knows of health.

When researching for this book I revisited old textbooks from university, college and school. I wanted to remind myself of all the interesting snippets of information that inspired me to learn more, so that I could echo them into the future. I decided that I wanted this book to be informative but also interesting and useful for everyday health, in the way some books are not.

Health as a subject is a broad spectrum. I wrote a lot of content for this book, but in the editing phase I realized health is too big a subject to swallow in one little book. So I have condensed what I had into what I think will be an interesting and useful read, instead of overwhelming the reader by pretending how smart I am. Therefore this isn't a comprehensive A–Z of health; instead I've selected what I think are the essentials and covered them. I plan to write a series of books so that I can express the full health spectrum in future volumes.

I warn you from the beginning this book contains opinions from a professional who isn't in anyone's pocket; I have studied conventional routes, of which I have drawn my own judgements. An old saying I follow is 'Wrong is wrong even if everyone is doing it and right is right even if no one is doing it'. Like everyone else I feel fear but I am not led by fear, and as Gandhi said, 'Even if you are in a minority of one, the truth is the truth'.

Without sounding too much like JFK, I have strong ideas about the current state of healthcare, I have strong ideas about how we can improve healthcare and I have strong ideas about how health as subject is as important as maths and science. I assure you my opinions are cross-referenced with holistic principles and with values of forgiveness, tolerance and kindness.

What I am offering here is personal reflections on my own learning from study, vocational experience and common sense. I am not a theorist author; this is not a book by an academic or a journalist who has no experience within the health industry. My skin has been in the game from nearly 20 years of working firstly as a personal trainer and now as a practitioner, running successful businesses, I might add. What is written within these pages I assure you is valid pragmatically and morally.

The style and perspective of this book is directed at readers within the UK. I welcome people from outside the UK reading this book but please forgive me for using colloquial terms and phases. If I am boasting about myself or being self-deprecating then in all likelihood I am joking. I am attempting to follow some sage advice by not taking myself too seriously. This means where appropriate I've used humour throughout the book. In my own learning, I learn best when it's fun, with creative analogies.

While we're on creative concepts, I'm afraid this isn't a real school; this is only a concept I thought up to make this book more interesting. However that does not mean that I am not open to creating a real health school in the future. If anyone else feels strongly about developing collective knowledge of our health then feel free to contact me on social media platforms (@ thebackdoctoruk) and I will be an advocate for your ideas.

Breaking into heaven

Lastly, before moving on I would like to state my position in terms of religion and spirituality so Stoical Beingism, the premise of chapter one (Philosophy), has more meaning as to why this concept exists. My own spiritual lineage begins with being born into religion, which I enjoyed emotionally but felt understimulated intellectually. I felt suffocated by the forcefulness to believe the symbolism was a fact and I couldn't understand as a youngster why the format and what the priest said was the same every week. Nothing evolved, which took the laws of nature out of the teachings for me.

As a young man I turned away from religion and I experimented with atheism. For a time I believed life had no meaning and that when we die we die, that the idea of an afterlife was folly and for the foolish. Organised religion never fulfilled me but neither did adopting an atheist viewpoint. I found rationalism to be as suffocating intellectually as religion. There is infinitely more that we do not know but I found people with this world view would construct a pretence that what was known disproved the unknown. I found this ironic because this is only a belief in the same way that religion is. To me they became polar opposites of one another, both partisan, unable to see either point of view like two fanatical football fans. The truth came second to protecting their identity and world view.

A turning point for me on my spiritual journey was the realisation that we all live within a construct of a belief system regarding spiritual matters, which cannot be proved by the means available to us today but more significantly cannot be disproved. Followers of a religion are only following a set of beliefs, as are atheists; therefore my spiritual awakening began with an acceptance of the unknown and a surrender to an infinitely complex universe, that I am only a tiny part of a greater intelligent power, which cannot be explained or described and is personal to me; and however small my part is, I am glad to be a part. Then in moment of inspired inspiration I felt fulfilled and Stoical Beingism as a philosophy was formed.

This made me a believer in an afterlife: I am the universe in human form, an expression of nature, and when I die I will go back to the universe. If I exist in an afterlife, logic makes sense to me that I existed before I was conceived. I am talking about spirit, the premise of all religions and people's compulsion to believe in such an abstract idea since the beginning of our existence. The repetition of coincidences in my life led me to construct a world view of an infinite interconnected reality, so complex than the finite human brain can only imagine its complexities.

Paperback Everest

I cannot speak for other authors, although I can tell you about my own experience of writing a book. My first attempt was like hanging around Everest base camp with a view to one day climbing to the top. I had a fear that on my ascent I would not be good enough to reach the top, returning to base camp on an oxygen mask, suffering with altitude sickness.

Due to my inexperience of writing I felt altitude sickness many times on my first attempt, but I am persistent in nature and I was determined to reach my Everest. As they say, we learn more from our failures than our successes. I was filled with limiting beliefs, namely that I wasn't good enough to write a book because at school I perceived myself to be rubbish at English. I based the rest of my life's ability on a few years in an education system that I know now suits the few and not the many.

I know schooling has improved since my days and I welcome that, but my experience of a learning style centred on comprehension was difficult to say the least. I was slow at skills they value the most such as reading, writing and listening. I would improvize by covering up my inability, pretending I knew what I was reading or hearing because I feared I would be in trouble if they knew. Looking back I was probably suffering with cerebellum underdevelopment, which I've since overcome.

Through reflecting on my own learning cycles I came to the conclusion beyond doubt that I am a kinesiology-based learner. I learn best through play and making subjects fun and exciting and in doing so I'm known for being a visionary, an original and free thinker. In the past when I was required to write an essay, those strengths would disappear and I was always filled with dread. I looked at essays as something to get through instead of enjoying learning about the topic of the essay.

For these reasons I found learning at school and educational settings to be rigid, with a lack of real-world relevance and impact. I left school with a filter (a concept explained in psychology/self-help manuals) of an aversion to education and learning. This textbook, if I call this book that, I hope will break these limiting beliefs for others, by presenting the content in a way that is easy to follow and interesting, while being fun but also profound. I wrote this book with my younger self in mind.

If at first we don't succeed...

When I started my first book I would write a passage that wouldn't make sense, or I'd screw up or miss the point and digress a lot. However, with time I got better at writing – by that I mean I got better and quicker at making points, structuring and editing my own work. Or probably a truer statement is I started to enjoy the writing process more.

I can best describe my improvement in writing the same way that someone might learn a language. Initially they learn the basics of pronunciation and comprehension of words, which enables them to develop into being able to participate in a conversation. Regardless of how gifted someone is with languages, to reach this stage takes time and repeated learning cycles.

What I learnt is that people commonly say one day they will write a book but never do, not because they can't or because of a lack of time, but because of the fear that people will think what they will write will be rubbish (guilty). They have an attitude of 'if it's not perfect, then don't do it at all' – why risk the embarrassment? I ruminated over these thoughts, they tied me up in knots – in pursuit of perfection – and then I knew what writer's block was.

Inspiration would return and I could write for hours, which in time resulted in a book that felt like a piece of art to me. People who read my first book gave me feedback and said my style was from the heart, easy to grasp and inspiring. I liked that. I never set out to develop a style but to know what I wrote was inspiring them to make better lifestyle choices was worth the effort.

Those same people would tell me they had begun walking or running regularly (from previously being inactive), they had made changes to their diet and in those moments I knew my first book, that was never intended to be a literal masterpiece, was doing what I set out to do.

I had a patient who's a long distance trucker and he bought my book. The next time I saw him I asked with anticipation what he thought and he said disappointingly that he had only read a few pages and left the book in a truck from which he was moved. He then said the next guy that drove this truck picked up my book and said he thought this was a load of rubbish at first. I feigned indifference to hide my sensitive side but then he surprised me as he went on to say that this other trucker had read most of the book and had made many changes to his diet and exercise habits.

Inspired by the chapter 'eat your medicine' he had also influenced his fellow truckers to buy gas stoves so that they could eat well on the road and that they were sharing the pictures of their food they cooked with each other. These chain events only happened as a result of my patient losing my book. It was a nice feeling to know someone I had never met had read my book and not only had they made changes in their life, they had helped others to do the same. It was a confirmation of my constructed world view that everything happens for a reason and made me hopefully that if this ripple effect gained momentum the world would undoubtedly change for the better.

I realized that when I wanted to write another book my goal would be 1) make the process fun to write 2) to use humour 3) to make what I wrote inclusive to anyone who wants to learn about their health, in the way medical textbooks do not. I wanted to tell the story of health essentials for people, without someone needing to enrol on a college or degree course in biology.

The good news about successfully climbing a metaphorical Everest is that the second time, I knew it was possible.

Mountain guides

There are some people I'd like to mention, who were integral mountain guides along the way. First are my parents, for their never-ending support on my journey of self-discovery. I am blessed my parents are role models of stoicism. They were born into working-class families that knew a scarcity which the generations of today in the UK can only imagine. They lived hand to mouth, but like their parents before them, in their hardship they never lost their dignity. My granddad went to school without any shoes, but he didn't know any different.

I'm blessed by my mum's kindness and eternal encouragement and advice. When I was younger Dad was my encyclopaedia; in my world there was nothing he didn't know if I asked him. Their wisdom and kindness inspire me. I am forever in their debt as I would not exist had it not been for the love and wisdom they created together. They consider themselves small people but they are the biggest people I know.

Throughout writing this book I took inspiration from *The Hitchhiker's Guide to The Galaxy*. It was such a great story and a thoughtful, inspiring sci-fi book of adventure, philosophy, maths and twisted logic; making fun of the oddness of the universe and the arbitrary rules we place on ourselves and others. Without sounding pompous, I've tried to recapture in my own style, the magic of *HGTTG* here. It even suggested a potential name for the book – *The Hitchhiker's Guide to Health* – but I preferred to start my own school, which is probably even more pompous!

I read *A Short History of Nearly Everything* by Bill Bryson about ten years ago or so and since then I've gone on to read most of his books. I liked his informal, self-deprecating style of writing, and his sprinkles of humour are genius. Humour with information, I believe, is the best way to learn. He is an excellent storyteller and I can't recommend his books highly enough.

Paul Chek is another person who has influenced my thinking. He is the first person I can ever remember using a Swiss ball – and look how common they are now; it would be unusual to walk into a gym and not see them. Before Paul's influence, the fitness industry was all Arnold machines, to isolate muscle groups, whereas he shifted the focus more towards the core and functional fitness, integrating multiple muscle group movements. All the functional training that is commonplace today was routed through Paul Chek and he doesn't get nearly enough credit in my opinion. In my mind he was ahead of his time and still is, with an understanding of science, philosophy and spirituality.

I also hold him in high esteem because we share a similar career lineage as he served in the US Army. He's been a good role model, by showing people like me they can be successful in other areas of life after the military. He is very intelligent but he doesn't make that smart person mistake that most do, when they claim to know everything through rational means only, disproving a higher power or holding that anything without evidence is nonsense. Intelligence and spirituality are more aligned than opposed to each other in my opinion.

While on the subject of science and spirituality, another inspiration of mine is Rupert Sheldrake. He is a modern-day genius and deserves to be as well known as Einstein. He is a rational scientist but what makes him so refreshing is he is not limited by the rational scientific model, as he is open to spirituality. His work on morphic resonance proposes that nature has a memory and is likely to be the next step in understanding evolution through the scientific model, which I will touch on in the microbiology section.

Another scientific monk is Bruce Lipton, who is the pioneer of epigenetics, which is scientific proof that our genes do not control our destiny; instead, our beliefs, emotions and environment do. Although there are some genetic diseases that pass at birth through family genes, there are no genes activated at birth for heart disease or cancer; instead they are activated throughout our lifetime and are usually triggered by lifestyle and stress. It's a profound scientific and philosophical shift that is still filtering through modern science and healthcare systems.

When I was younger I liked Oasis, with their feel-good Beatle-esque pop/rock music and their punk attitude. I identified with them as people because I am from a working-class background and of mixed heritage, like most of the band. Their appearance of a lack of fame-hunger and their abstinence from people-pleasing appealed to me.

I couldn't explain this at the time but on reflection in their youthful pomp, they represented a new British-ness to me that if someone believed in themselves and they were good enough, anything was possible. This new mindset doesn't need you to sell out to achieve your dreams.

Oasis were never going to be the new faces of McDonald's (Justin Timberlake), the perfume Brut (Vinny Jones) or Coca Cola (Marcus Rashford). While holding the government to account on free lunches, Marcus Rashford is also helping to ensure that children are given a packet of sweets and a fizzy drink before every class, in support of the Ironic Policies Act 2022.

I liked to think that even if Noel Gallagher was broke, he'd rather busk on the street than put his name to something he didn't believe in. I made a private vow a long time ago that I am making public here; I will never encourage a product or service that does not fit within my values or principles, regardless of the incentive.

Anyhow, I'm digressing again – I didn't say I was any good at writing, I just said I enjoyed the process.

Prospectus

This is a letter of congratulations! You've been awarded a scholarship at the The Back Doctor's prestigious School of Health. Included in this letter is your textbook with all the topics we be covering on this course. I am David Tennison and I will be your teacher. To share a bit about myself, I am a former Royal Marine, with previous experience of running my own personal training business. I have worked within the NHS as an exercise professional; I've also spent half a decade studying for a master's degree in chiropractic and on the publication of this book, I will have been practising for nearly eight years. Yes, I've been busy.

The concept of this book is: if health was a subject at school, what would it look like? It seems logical to me that if someone inspected a bridge, we would want someone experienced and trained in knowing how prevent the bridge from falling into disrepair. We are all inspectors of our own bridges. I aim on this course to help people to inspect their own health, mentally and physically, so they can act before disease begins. It make sense to me that if we own a body, then learning about our health is a must, in the same way that we manage our finances, take our car for a service or brush our teeth regularly, so that we can prevent the loss of health and maintain wellness.

Currently within our healthcare model we wait for the bridge to fall into disrepair before even considering taking action. The medical profession which controls healthcare sees a person without symptoms as being healthy. In most cases they will only inspect a patient once they develop some kind of health issue, although symptoms when they arise are the tip of the iceberg. The longer we wait for symptoms to arise, the more likely medication is the only solution. The time has passed to manage the condition with lifestyle modifications only.

Dis-ease before disease

Underneath the tip of the iceberg of disease is a period of time called dis-ease, which is psychological ill health, and in most cases precipitates physical disease. Dis-ease is a term from the early 20th century that has lost its meaning because healthcare in the 21st century has no adequate capacity to measure psychological ill health. This is where lifestyle modifications can not only stop the progression but people can make a full recovery. Areas needed for inspection in dis-ease are shown opposite.

These are markers of our health, and when they are addressed and restored, they are similar to changing a washer and bolt on a bridge, preventing a closure of the bridge for repair.

The smoking gun of big business

My first book was dedicated to explaining the cause of why we are being short changed by a public-funded healthcare system, which plays into the hands of pharmaceutical companies. Instead of our taxes being spent on keeping us healthy, they are being spent on letting us become sick; and then when we are sick our health is predominately managed by pharmaceutical medication and given stigmatized diagnostic labels. A scientifically proven, proactive wellness model driven by lifestyle modification that would prevent many diseases is being suppressed because there is less profit in you being healthy.

In my first book I used the example of how cigarette companies with vested interests in the 1960s created a body of scientific evidence to support counterclaims to the suggestion that their products caused lung cancer. This campaign slowed anti-smoking legislation by an estimated 20 years. A similar practice happened more recently with car manufacturers, which had R&D departments present the appearance of researching electric cars but had no interest in developing them because of the effect this shift away from combustion engines would have on their existing business model. They only made the shift when open patents were developed and their bluff was called.

Big bossiness has a track record of appearing to be working

Dis-ease Before Disease

Underneath the tip of the iceberg of disease is a period of time called dis-ease, which is psychological ill health, precipitating physical disease. This is where lifestyle modifications can not only stop the progression but people can make a full recovery. Areas needed for inspection in dis-ease:

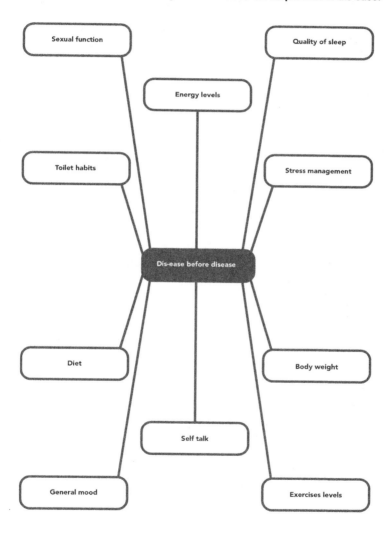

in everyone's best interests but secretly they are working ruthlessly to their own agenda. The pharmaceutical companies are no different, slowing the momentum of natural healthcare innovations to protect their own business models, supported by the healthcare system.

The miracle of the human body

Inside every human is a collection of complex individual biological factories (cells) producing millions of chemical reactions every second that add up to your health. The word 'healthy' split into two is *heal* and *thy*; this translates into old English meaning 'you heal' (from an original Germanic word meaning 'whole'), therefore healthy means that our body is constantly healing. We often take for granted our body's continuous ability to heal or we are totally unaware of these life forces. They are individual working parts that come together to form systems of organs, producing remarkable stats that usually begin from you're the moment we are born till the day we die.

Function	Day	Year	Life
Thoughts	100K	36.52M	2.92B
Breaths	20K	7.3M	584M
Heart beats	100K	36.5M	2.29B
Blinking	16.8K	6.132M	490.560M
Swallowing	600	219K	17.52M
Sneezing	4	1.46K	116.8K
Yawning	20	7.3K	584K
Steps	10K	3.65M	292M
Eat	1.6kg	596kg	47682kg
Sleep	8	2.92K	233.6K
Awake	16	5.84K	467.2K
Calories	2.25K	821.25K	65.7M

By the end of the today your heart will have pumped 6,000–7,500 litres of blood around 25,000 km of blood vessels. Our hearts will maintain a steady beat throughout the day (an average of 100,000 beats per day) and will increase the rate to keep up with the demands of the body. There is no carrot or stick needed, no need for a motivational speech; our heart and other organs are loyal obedient servants. In the same time frame, your lungs will have sucked in 11,000 litres of air from the atmosphere to supply the heart with oxygenated blood.

Millions of organized red blood cells will pick up oxygen and drop off carbon dioxide at the lungs without any consideration other than how can they be more efficient. In turn they will provide trillions of cells that cling together to make one whole human being with oxygen. Our kidneys will produce on average 1.7 litres of urine daily to filter our blood of toxins and waste.

Average Human	Count
Hairs	5M
Joints	360
Bones	206
Muscles	600
Ligaments	900
Tendons	4K
Body weight in water	60-70%

That food we just ate is being separated by one the oldest part of our genetic heritage, the digestive system. As you will find out in subsequent chapters, the digestive system was the first system to evolve and, like the heart and lungs, is efficient on its own account, separating all the constituent parts of our meal, so they can be digested for energy, growth and repair at a cellular level. The digestive system even has its own nervous system, which can warn us of danger and is in tune (notice the similarity of the word 'intuition' with 'in tune') with our environment, commonly known as our gut feeling.

Thanks to 37 km of nerves, you are able to coordinate these many tasks simultaneously, some consciously, but the majority subconsciously. Similar to a programmed computer over time, we can learn tasks and become so good at them that we can multitask, such as simultaneously walking and talking. Even when we are asleep there is no need to set a timer – our heart will still beat, our lungs still breathe, we will still digest food. Just because we are asleep doesn't mean that life forces stop. The subconscious innate forces will look after these essential tasks for us.

We, the observers, will only ever question these innate life forces if they stop working or they go wrong for whatever reason. This book will help us understand these life forces and how we can proactively support them to prevent them from going wrong.

Themes and concepts

This book will fill in the missing gaps in our educational system, without getting too stuffy or technical (phew! I hear a few of you say) but still being relevant and interesting. Too often within a learning setting, the information is more complicated than needed, is not in a bite-sized format or is presented too drily.

If you're new to learning about health, this book is a perfect start or, perhaps, if you're already at Einstein level on health matters, this book will reinforce your current knowledge and understanding. I see this book as offering the broad strokes for health and a stepping stone to further understanding, while also presenting non-mainstream ideas and a fresh perspective. I do not see those perspectives as right or wrong; I would rather consider them as breaking the rules of conventional thinking to manifest new understanding and develop further questions.

For us to progress in health and wellness it's not about increasing knowledge of a few studied experts, it's about helping the majority of us to understand our own health and make it interesting enough that we want to learn more.

I will be presenting ideas for your consideration that might come as a surprise because of the limited knowledge we are taught about our health. These ideas might feel far out there, but if you're prepared to follow me down the rabbit hole then you might reach the same conclusions. I'm going to present original ideas I've developed myself and the work of others with my interpretation.

Aims of this book

My aim is to convey the following ideas:

→ Health is a subject as critical for students to understand as English, languages, maths and science. A focus on health education would encourage individuals to take personal responsibility for their own health so that instead of waiting until they become sick, they can prevent ill health through knowledge, exercise, diet and mindset. This book aims to put together the essentials, minus the gimmicks suited to a particular industry's influence and patronage. Good health is easier and simpler than most people realize.

→ Stoical Beingism is my name for a collection of philosophies from sages of the past, updated so that the teachings are meaningful for our time. The premise is that health is not just about the individual – our health is a collective thing. When we consider our own health we must consider the environment and ecosystems, and view all life as significant as human life. We must also acknowledge our feelings but we must not become a victim to them.

→ Life is conscious and intelligent at every level of existence. I think it's a conceit of scientists to say with authority that below the conscious mind there is no consciousness. Consider a sperm for a moment, swimming towards an egg and starting the process of procreation. It makes sense to me that there is intelligence in these single-celled organisms. Orthodox scientists says this is just chemistry, with no intelligence or consciousness; I will present counterarguments to the contrary.

→ I will hold a mirror up to how the body works and compare it with the current healthcare model to show the disparity between the two. Our healthcare system waits until a

31

person is sick before acting, which in many cases is too late, as disease reaches past the point of prevention. Healthcare at present does not encourage our body's natural healing capability as result. When people become sick, the time for holistic lifestyles solutions has usually passed and pharmaceutical medication is therefore perceived to be the only option.

→ I will show the dominant philosophy within healthcare is unevenly balanced towards mechanistic and not holistic solutions, which again supports the use of pharmaceutical interventions. These can cause more damage than profit to individual health because of their poisonous nature and intention. This encourages an 'outside-in' mindset in the practitioner and patient (explained in the philosophy section later) that health is a commodity which can be manufactured by industrial medication, or that these medications control dials and levers like a machine in the body.

→ I will introduce the Hybrid Practitioner. These evidenced-based healers will be the future of healthcare, providing a split skill set, part physician and part psychologist. Instead of being only rational, scientific and symptom focused, Hybrid Practitioners will able to heal their patients mentally, physically and emotionally. They will be able to touch the part of their patient where the underlying cause is and resolve the issue before any medication is prescribed or considered because of their understanding of patient psychology.

→ I will dedicate a chapter to practical physical education, centred on developing fitness as a progression and how to prevent and limit injuries when and if they occur. I will give advice on good forms of household chores such as gardening and hovering, and for common problems like sitting, to limit and prevent injury. The Hybrid Practitioner will also offer a self-help guiding framework for improving towards fully functioning mentally and physically.

→ I will teach the basics of psychology. How managing our

emotions is a lifelong task, best acted upon before crisis point. How our mental health problems, when unresolved, can be the cause of physical symptoms and unwonted behaviors. Instead of a focus on mental loss of health only at crisis point, I will focus on managing or regaining mental balance and wellness as a lifetime solution.

The Back Doctor Pyramid

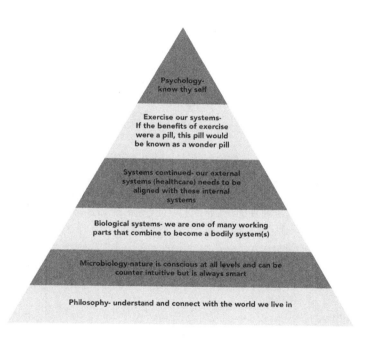

The reason this book exists is because health is not taught as a subject. The closest understanding of the spectrum of health in our tradition educational setting is biology or sexual education. The former isn't taught with a holistic overview and the latter is a reaction to an increase in teenage pregnancies. We need a new, proactive, holistic approach to teach health to future generations.

At the end of each chapter I've added a quiz to test the skimming readers were paying attention. All the answers can be found in the chapters and are informative and in places intentionally humorous. I've also deliberately left the answers out to make you think instead of giving the answer instantly.

I'll give you an example why. I was in a pub reading a book once and I asked this guy if he knew the meaning of a word in my book and he mutely immediately reached for his phone to find the answer, with no discussion or deliberation on this word's possible meaning. The discussion was more significant to me than the gratification of the answer. The conclusion you draw through your own thinking will more likely improve your cognitive function than technology concluding for you.

Use the questions to discuss the answers with others for further understanding and clarification. You might find a truth that I missed.

The magic intervention

There is a magic pill proven beyond doubt that will help with improve your health regardless of your health issues, mental and physical, which has also been shown to **reduce all-cause mortality.** Taken consistently this pill will solve the real pandemic of obesity and will beat other medication hands down like anti-depression and pain medication. The science has shown that this pill outperforms and is superior to any other prescribed medication. And what's more, this medication, in comparison to other treatments, when prescribed within the patient's limits, has **no side effects.**

What is this scientifically proven and validated wonder pill, you ask? **Regular exercise.** You might be scratching your head at the moment – if this is true, why is this is not on billboards and shouted from rooftops? Does it cost too much? (It's more cost effective than pharmaceutical medication.) Is it too difficult to recommend to everyone? (The only requirement is an assessment to recommend exercise within a person's limits.) Ask yourself this question: if you didn't know that exercise was the magic pill, what else is being kept from you that's in your interest?

I'm not pretending to know all the answers to our healthcare problems in this book. I am merely presenting the essentials of health and new ideas that are worthy of consideration towards a proactive healthcare model that would serve the public better than the current reactionary model.

With reference to the famous Pink Floyd song, it's time to transcend the bricks of the wall and to end this thought control.

It's time to start the course, so when you're ready... let's go back to school.

And I kindly ask if everyone could head to the assembly hall for the course opening ceremony.

Examples of **all-cause mortality** which regular exercise will not only help to prevent but will also slow the progression of these diseases

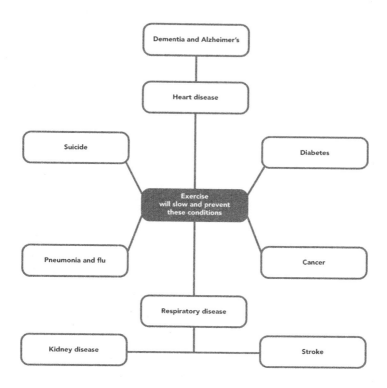

David Tennison's opening address

For the opening address of this course I would like to quote a speech by Charlie Chaplin from his film *The Great Dictator*. He needs no introduction but we will provide one for this extraordinary gentleman, as from humble beginnings he became a prodigious star of the silver screen but through this pomp of stardom he never sold out, and he never betrayed the principles of liberty and humanity.

Charlie never gave in, he never compromised on his humanitarian principles, and he stood up against intense pressure for what he believed in, which makes him an inspiration in my book, pun intended. In his time he was loved by the little people but hated by so-called representatives of established institutions of society because he did not conform to their questionable ideology based on fear.

His art is a timeless odyssey of comedy and tragedy, which enriched the world with happiness and empathy. We are blessed that a gentle soul as he ever lived, and was able to reach us through noise of fear and consumerism.

'I'm sorry but I don't want to be an Emperor. That's not my business. I don't want to rule or conquer anyone. I should like to help everyone if possible – Jew, Gentile – black man – white.

We all want to help one another – human beings are like that. We all want to live by each other's happiness, not by each other's misery. We don't want to hate and despise one another. In this world there is room for everyone and the good earth is rich and can provide for everyone.

The way of life can be free and beautiful. But we have lost the way. Greed has poisoned men's souls, has barricaded the world with hate, has goose-stepped us into misery and bloodshed. We have developed speed but we have shut ourselves in: machinery that gives abundance has left us in want. Our knowledge has made us cynical, our cleverness hard and unkind. We think too much and feel too little: more than machinery we need humanity; more than cleverness we need kindness and gentleness. Without these qualities, life will be violent and all will be lost.

The *aeroplane* and the *radio* have brought us closer together. The very nature of these inventions cries out for the goodness in *men*, cries out for universal brotherhood for the unity of us all. Even now my voice is reaching millions throughout the world, millions of despairing men, women and little children, victims of a system that makes *men* torture and imprison innocent people. To those who can hear me I say, "Do not despair". The misery that is now upon us is but the passing of greed, the bitterness of men who fear the way of human progress. The hate of men will pass and the power they took from the people will return to the people and liberty will never perish.

Soldiers! Don't give yourself to these brutes – who despise you – enslave you – who regiment your lives – tell you what to do – what to think and what to feel! Who drill you – diet you – treat you like cattle and sue you as cannon fodder. Don't give yourselves to these unnatural *men* – machine *men* with machine minds and machine hearts! You are not machines! You are men! With the love of humanity in your hearts! Don't hate! Only the unloved hate – the unloved and the unnatural!

In the seventeenth chapter of Saint Luke it is written, "The kingdom of God is within man." Not one man, nor a group of men, but in all men – in you, the people. You the people have the power, the power to create machines, the power to create happiness. You the people have the power to make life free and beautiful, to make this life a wonderful adventure. Then in the name of democracy let's use that power.

Let us all unite. Let us fight for a new world, a decent world that will give men a chance to work that will give you the future and old age and security. Let us fight to free the world, to do away with national barriers, do away with greed, with hate and intolerance. Let us fight for a world of reason, a world where science and progress will lead to all men's happiness. Let us all unite!

Wherever you are, look up! The clouds are lifting! The sun is breaking through! We are coming out of the darkness into the light! We are coming into a new world – a kindlier world, where people will rise above their greed, their hate and their brutality. Look up, *students!* The soul of *man* has been given wings and at last he is beginning to fly. *He is* flying into the rainbow – into the light of hope. Look up! Look up!'

This extract is from the book Charles Chaplin, My Autobiography, *chapter twenty-five, which is the closing speech of his timeless feature film* The Great Dictator, 1940. *Copyright © Roy Export S.A.S. Reproduced with permission.*

.

Philosophy

Welcome

If everyone would please take a seat in the assembly hall, we will begin this course with a ceremony, offering thanks and praise to all that we are blessed with. The Back Doctor School of Health does not attach itself to any organized religion but is respectful of adherents of all faiths. We see the value in believing in a cause bigger than ourselves. When we are overly focused on our own needs, we forget the value of teamwork towards a combined interest of a greater good and the age-old truth that some are far worse off than us.

This school respects individual freedoms, by encouraging autonomous and self-directive behaviour. There are no mistakes, only learning through reflection and refining, helping people to make a better choice next time because they want to, not because they are told to. Instead of seeking revenge, retribution or punishment, we seek first to understand and then forgive, before judging. All students are equal to one another, as we practise a live-and-let-live attitude, we encourage students to accept each other's differences while also uniting on our similarities.

What is a philosophy?

A philosophy is a set of principles and values based on plausible assumptions, followed by a sequence of logical proven or unproven conclusions, where those unproven conclusions cannot be disproved. Some philosophies are more relevant than others, standing the test of time. With enough thought and effort, anyone can develop a philosophy of their own. The world according to The Back Doctor School of Health is a collection of timeless philosophies, combined together so that the teachings are updated and relevant to our modern age.

Our philosophy is 'Stoical Beingism', which is an extension of humanism, combined with secular spiritualism, in the sense that we use the spiritual teachings of religion, without the dogmas or literal interpretation. We do not believe anyone goes to hell after death, but we are open to the idea of an afterlife where we live on beyond the limitations of the human form, known as spirit.

Never heard of Stoical Beingism? Don't worry, it's because it's something I've made up! It's not a religion but a potential spiritual and political movement, using the wisdom of religion without needing to attach to a specific one. It's also an understanding that all life is sacred, whether it is a flower, a tree or an insect, all life is as important as the next, as are people's views and choices. It's a management system for processing emotions to maintain our mental wellness.

This is a philosophy in the best interest of a balanced greater good, instead of the greater good of organisations such as big business. It is the greater good that respects nature, uses resources wisely and places individual power over absolute power. It's a pragmatic approach, with consideration to us and others. It's a broad-scope philosophy that everyone can live by without exception, taking on the wisdom of our ancestors and the natural world.

Followers of religion need not fear as Stoical Beingism is no threat to the tenets of religion; instead this philosophy will be complimentary with their beliefs. Think of this philosophy as a knitting needle with the ability to thread all religions together, uniting them for a common cause.

As much as we want to control our environment and our surroundings, nature has its own set of rules. Natural laws are not written down like formal religions, relevant to a particular stage of civilisation of the past, and in doing so locking rules in time as dogmas, so that when technology and philosophies evolve they lose their meaning. Natural laws are self-evident, inalienable truths, timeless principles, maintaining their relevance since their inception (long before human inception). They are based on laws of ecology, cooperation, growth and entropy, that one day we will die as everything in nature is meant to do, making way for the new.

Science is proving that animals and plants experience emotions and that they are also conscious. Human beings are an exceptional species, – as far as we can tell we are the only child of nature to develop analytical thinking and a reflective conscious consciousness. This is an achievement but it's also a responsibility to be the guardians of Earth, not just for us or for other species, but also for nature as a whole.

The philosophy of Stoical Beingism:

→ **Live and let live**: the code of the School is to be tolerant of other people's views and avoid prejudices that would intentionally hurt or hold others back, while also honoring liberty over restrictions. When we meet resistance to our world view, always seek first to understand and then be understood. Build bridges for those stuck in dogmas or polarized views, so if they choose, they can be liberated from their limiting belief systems that do not serve them or a greater good. Self-evaluate non-judgmentally. Show compassion to yourself and others.

→ **All beings are equal**: respect sacrifice, nature and freedom over regulation. When we strip back human technology, abstract thought and all the rules created by society, we see that each of us is just another being of planet Earth, which is as much about other life forms as it is about our own. Ecosystems that allow life to flourish and their habitats are being removed at record rates. It's in our interest to protect these ecosystems, because of the symbiotic relationship we share with nature. We are already in the Garden of Eden.

→ **Offer gratitude to the universe**: We only exist because a host of chance variables allow the conditions on Earth to be suitable for life. Secular scientists and atheists believe it's just random chance, plain good luck that we exist, without any recognition of a connecting or higher power in the universe. That's fine, I understand that world view, but the problem is that there is no one to thank, or a reason to be here in their version of creation. It makes sense to me that there is intelligence and creativity in the universe, therefore whatever that intelligence is (non-religious) I offer thanks for living and breathing.

→ **Health is a blessing**: if you are able bodied with the ability to make self-determined choices and exercise free will, please consider there are always many others more disadvantaged us. Health is the single most valuable possession you will ever be blessed with. Some of us are born with health issues or they develop them over a life time. Health is a combination of all your working parts, working together in tandem and cooperation; even when we are asleep, these functions work for us. Support your life forces by exercising regularly and maintaining a health-focused mindset.

→ **Live in hope**: The serenity prayer is 'God give me the serenity to accept the things I cannot change, courage for the things I can and the wisdom to know the difference'. See the good in all — when someone wrongs you, think of a reason to thank them. Doing this is as much for you to let go than exercising forgiveness. Focus on what you can control not what is beyond your control. Rise above apathy by questioning. Optimism over pessimism. Be the change you want to see in the world. Hope for the best and plan for the worst.

→ **Big isn't always better**: natural over artificial and individual power over absolute power. We can act laterally globally with other nations but not at the expense of individual freedoms and the environment. Liberated people are more likely to further technology and raise consciousness than societies that are traditionally coerced by fear and dominated by absolute power. Support businesses in alignment with natural laws.

→ **Live ecologically**: use resources wisely, protect the environment and connect with nature. Climate change is one reason to reduce our carbon footprint and destruction of natural areas of beauty but being warned of a catastrophe to respect the planet is reactionary. Regardless of climate change we are morally obliged to use resources of the earth wisely and in accordance with natural laws.

→ **Live in peace and harmony (Christian values):** Avoid punishment, revenge and retribution. Give those that wrong us or others the benefit of doubt where possible. Aim to forgive all while putting boundaries in place so that we can forgive while not letting others that lack integrity take advantage of us again. Avoid fads, sensational news and fearmongering. Focus your energy on only speaking the good of others. Seek guidance from the timeless teachings of sages of the past, not influenced by modern fads and fashions. Do what brings you joy and peace.

→ **We are all one:** there is potentially a collective consciousness as outlined in Carl Jung's archetypes, which proposes we are all connected in our dream state. Japanese samurai would channel warrior spirits of the past by asking for inspiration, asking 'What would a great warrior do?' Rupert Sheldrake's morphic resonance is a scientifically proven concept that there is a cellular memory connecting not only with the present but also past generations.

→ **Winning at all costs is a lose-lose strategy:** absolute winning to crush or dominate an opponent without humility or compassion is always a lose-lose situation. A win-win solution is balancing the greater good with all the information available, satisfying all sides while also remaining pragmatic. Be competitive without being consumed by competiveness. Winning by unfair means, taking advantage of others, ripples through the generations in a timeless karma in this life or the next.

→ **A belief in a higher power is good for you:** people that believe in a power bigger than themselves are scientifically proven to be happier, healthier and live longer than people that do not. They are more grateful people and if it was a popularity contest they would win because they are proven to be more popular than non-believers.

45

The miracle of life only exists because the universe exists. We can only be in possession of health because of the cycle of life and death. Humans are a remarkable species, no doubt, but even we are just another branch of the tree of life. We are blessed to be here, as we will see...

Beingism

The ever-changing understanding of the universe

The story and the meaning of the universe has changed significantly since humans began walking the earth 80,000 years ago. Our hunter-gatherer ancestors buried their dead with ceremonial traditions, suggesting they believed in an offering to a higher power or the existence of an afterlife. In tribal life they would pray to God or gods in ceremony and dance, and use sacrifices, in the hope that in return food and water would be abundant and their loved ones would be healthy.

After the time of Jesus, Western culture shifted from the worship of nature to a story of creation, of a God in our image. Approximately 200 years after his death the teachings of Jesus were locked in time in texts in an attempt to unite Christianity and to provide a moral code for Christians to live by. This over time created rigid philosophical lines, open to interpretation and abuse; therefore, instead of uniting, Christianity would fracture into schisms.

Up until the Renaissance this story of the universe was unchallenged and ubiquitous. In this understanding of the universe, Earth was at the centre, with an afterlife in a parallel dimension. Then Darwin's theory of natural selection threw the cat amongst the pigeons. Extreme evolutionists went as far to say that evolution theory disproved there is a God or an afterlife.

Hubble's vision

The 20th century saw giant leaps in ideas and technology. The list is long one of human ingenuity, but near the top has to be the Hubble telescope. The telescope is named in honor of Edwin Hubble, who made groundbreaking discoveries to understand the dynamics of the universe at the beginning of the same century. Edwin Hubble made two significant discoveries that changed how we view the universe:

1. Before the 20th century, the Milky Way was thought to be the only galaxy in the universe. Hubble demonstrated not only are there bigger galaxies but they are more distant than anyone ever imagined. We now know of 140 billion galaxies, and that's only what we can see in the known universe.

2. The universe is inflating and expanding in all directions, instead of being a static shape and size. This gave rise to the theory of the Big Bang, that if the universe is inflationary, the beginning could be traced back to a beginning of time and space, where there was no time or space, just a primeval atom, smaller than a pinhead. This atom for reasons unknown 'decided' to expand and has been expanding ever since.

People figured this out through powerful telescopes, but there was a problem: scientists using the telescopes on Earth had to gaze through the atmosphere, which distorted the telescope's image. This limited how far could be seen, regardless of the telescopic magnification. The Hubble telescope suspended above the atmosphere in Earth's lower orbit solved this problem.

Bypassing the atmosphere, astronomers can see further than ever before – the universe has been opened up to us. The more we learn, the more distant we become from being the centre of the universe. In space, time and distance are inseparable. The Hubble telescope is able to look back into the distant past 14 billion years ago, to see the edge of our universe. With this profound information a new interpretation is needed for mankind.

The miracle of the solar system

To honour the lineage of survival of life on Earth for 3.8 billion years, so that we could be alive today, I think some special thanks are due, let's start with the Sun...

Around 4.6 billion years ago our Sun was born and although small for a star, the Sun is large enough to encase a million Earths. The Sun is a giant nuclear fusion reactor, with a surface temperature of 6000°C. At the birth of the Sun there was no order in the solar system – instead it was a chaotic vortex of gas and rock, for tens of thousands of millions of years. The Sun's gravity caused the debris of rock and gas to assemble together in similar orbits. Planets of dust and rock formed four of the inner worlds, known as the terrestrial planets, Mercury, Venus, Earth and Mars. Further out is Jupiter and the other gas giants, Saturn, Uranus and Neptune.

For the first billion or so years the Sun wasn't as bright as it is today because it was newly formed. The Sun we know today is mid-life and scientists predict our star of the solar system will eventually burn out in five billion years' time, as all stars are destined to do ultimately. From observing other stars we know in two billion years the Sun's surface will start to inflate, engulfing Mercury and Venus. At this point the Sun's temperature will increase, melting ice worlds that were once too far from the Sun to feel the effects of its heat.

The miracle of life on Earth

As far as we tell Earth is unique in the sense that life hasn't been found anyone else in our solar system or anywhere else in universe for that matter. When the first modern astronomers viewed Venus and Mars, they extrapolated that civilisation must be happening there too. Astronomers in the 19th century looked through their telescopes on to the surface of these planets and they thought they were seeing vegetation, canals and cities. Well into the 20th century, people would think these planets were inhabited by life. However, it wasn't to be, as space missions across the solar system would find. Life on Earth is therefore a miracle of sorts and a miracle most vital to us.

Earth is orbiting a star that's small enough to not burn itself out quickly; larger stars burn more intensely but for shorter periods. Life on Earth is blessed that it is a distance from the Sun that replenishes, rather than destroying our environment. This was the fate of Venus, the next planet closer than us to the Sun.

49

We are close enough to the Sun so that its warmth is beneficial and not too far away, so that our oceans do not freeze.

Venus

Venus is the same size as Earth but if you're ever thinking about a holiday there, think again, unless you're prepared to hold your breath for the entire trip, as Venus's atmosphere is 96% carbon dioxide. It's a great place for tan though, with a temperature of a cool 457°C. This is due to the greenhouse effect. Carbon dioxide has been trapping sunlight in the atmosphere as infrared heat for over billions of years, frying Venus.

If you were planning a visit to Venus then the best time to go would have been two billion years ago, before the greenhouse effect hit a tipping point of rising temperatures. It is thought in this period that Venus had oceans with an atmosphere of a mixture of greenhouse gases, much like Earth today. Even though Mercury is closer to the Sun than Venus, Venus is the hottest planet in the solar system because of the runaway effect of the greenhouse gases. If the solar system is a desert, then Earth is its oasis.

If a holiday to Venus isn't your thing, then maybe you'd consider Mars, but remember to bring a coat because, although Mars is still within a range from the Sun to sustain life, it is a cold, barren rock in comparison to Earth. But it wasn't always like that, as we are learning.

Mars

Within the last ten years Rover missions to Mars and probes monitoring the surface have concluded that a few billion years ago, Mars looked similar to Earth, with a thick atmosphere, oceans, river canyons bigger than the Grand Canyon and also the largest volcano ever found anywhere in the solar system. The conditions for complex life on Mars lasted for hundreds of millions of years and then, puff, they disappeared.

For whatever reason, after this period the atmosphere on Mars began to thin and as a consequence the water on Mars evaporated to be lost forever. The newest theory is when the core of Mars cooled the magnetic field weakened, which had maintained an atmosphere. Solar winds were able to penetrate the ground and strip away the conditions for complex life. It seems that being the correct range from the Sun is only one variable for sustaining life.

These worlds at some point were hospitable to life but for one reason or another conditions for complex life changed, whereas for four billion years, Earth has managed to maintain liquid water in the form of oceans and seas on her surface, allowing complex carbon chemistry to develop.

The Earth's atmosphere

Going back 3.5 billion years ago, Earth was Earth but not as we know it today. It was unrecognisable as the planet we call home. The atmosphere was thick with carbon dioxide and the oceans were acidic, making Earth more similar to that of Venus. We need to acknowledge those parts of life that breathe carbon dioxide because we are breathing the oxygen they expel.

Special thanks must therefore go to the atmosphere. Not only is our atmosphere filled with oxygen, essential for our survival, but air keeps us warm. Without air circulating around us the temperature would be −18°C, similar to the vacuum of space. The atmosphere also stops cosmic radiation, meteors and anything else that might do us harm. It is the reason why our planet has retained oceans and seas and how we can live on land.

Plant life and photosynthesis

If we must mention the atmosphere then we must mention algae, trees and plant life, as they are the reason our atmosphere is rich in oxygen. Before mammals even existed, trees were filling the atmosphere with oxygen, before our arrival. They pre-date the dinosaurs and it is thought that before our arrival, trees covered most of the land in what became Britain.

The algae in the oceans date back over 3.5 billion years ago. Their ability to photosynthesize carbon dioxide into oxygen is why oxygen is abundant and together with plants they capture three trillion kilowatts of solar energy from the Sun a day. This energy is then passed down through the food chains, of which we are in one of many.

The Moon

We also need a special thanks to the Moon, our night companion. The Moon is approximately a quarter of the size of the Earth. It's covered in craters to show how violent the universe once was. Its gravitational pull is so powerful that it creates ocean tides on Earth. The Moon's orbit stabilizes Earth's rotation on her axis . The world spins around neatly because of the Moon; no one knows what would happen if the Moon suddenly disappeared but by most accounts the options aren't good.

The theory of how the Moon came to be is that in the early life of Earth, a meteor storm hit Earth and a chunk of rock broke away and over time that became the Moon. No other terrestrial planet has a moon. They are normally only reserved for the bigger planets such as Jupiter or Saturn.

The layers of Earth

The Earth's core is also blessed with a centre as hot as the surface of the Sun. This self-perpetuating internal heating system is a dynamo, converting magnetic energy into heat. The Earth is surrounded by a magnetic field that protects us from already mentioned harmful solar winds from the Sun. If Earth was without a magnetic field they would burst through and life might never have got started in the first place. It would appear that the Earth is alive just as we are.

Earth's crust is its outer surface, the skin if you like, and similar to our skin, the crust is constantly regenerating – in this case through volcanic activity, changes in weathering, oceans and the regeneration of tectonic plates. The Earth swallows ground between tectonic plates and in its place new land is pushed upwards. This is how geologists can tell the age of fossils from the layer of sediment they find.

You may be surprised that mountains like Mount Everest are relatively new additions to our landscapes. Tectonic plates move underneath us and they push together, and when they do they force ground upwards and voila, a mountain appears. Those mountains need some love too because they form part of our weather system. Water evaporates, making clouds, which spray our lands for plants and wildlife to flourish. They create river networks for wildlife and were vital for early settlements.

The abundance of water

Let's take a moment to consider the absolute essentialness of water. Most of the world is covered in oceans, seas, lakes and rivers. Water constitutes 60-70% of all mammals, and the same for most vegetables and fruit. Our cells are bathed in water. If water or food became scarce we would die of dehydration before hunger. That's probably why when we are parched, water tastes so good. Water truly is abundant on Earth, and thank goodness too.

What does this all mean regarding our health?

We are a product of Earth, within a solar system powered by the Sun, in a galaxy called the Milky Way, within an infinite universe. The environment did not adapt to us, we adapted to the environment. Had photosynthesis been to discharge carbon dioxide we would probably evolved to breathe CO_2 instead of oxygen or not have evolved at all.

Our health is only possible because this chain of events on Earth, over a period of 4 billion years, allow us to be alive, to consider an abstract idea, called health. We are just organized stardust of the universe and when it's all over and we will die, and the stardust that was once us will form another object or being. Therefore health is not only abstract but is time limited.

The Earth's biodiverse ecosystems and resources which we are a part of are not infinite. By using those resources unwisely and unsustainably, we are removing nature's habitats at a risk to our shared ecosystem.

So yes, when we talk about our health we need to discuss our insides and how our bodies work, but we also need to orientate ourselves to the outside world in which we live. **Health is not just an individual thing; health is collective.**

In our modern age we are conditioned to not think holistically about the world, but as we are seeing with global warming and the extinction of great species of the African savannahs, we are in need of a philosophical re-evaluation, both as individuals and as a collective. To do that we need to look around and ask questions, and start thinking for ourselves instead of allowing big business and governments to do this for us. As individuals we need to improve our own understanding of the natural laws of the universe so we can support them instead of hindering them.

Stoicism

Family run businesses vs big business

When people question whether climate change is real, I always say that even if it is not, it's sensible to use the world's resources ecologically. Or put another way: is gambling our environment worth the risk? We are consumers in society but is consumerism out of control and if so what steps could we collective take to make society in alignment with a sustainable environment?

We are all born into a system that already exists, known as society, which has predetermined obligations such as legal, moral and financial expectations. How we feel about these systems will depend on our social class, gender, ethnicity, faith and personal experiences. Those systems are made up by humans of the past and present in an attempt to make sense of the world. They are not set in stone, they are not forever, and they are just the chosen way at present.

By questioning these systems we are able to reflect and refine on them so that **the next generation of people can continue farming on fertile soil, not depleted by fertilizers, be protected by an ozone layer, breathe fresh unpolluted air, and be able to access fresh drinking water and food without chemicals. We take all of these natural environmental products of the Earth's ecosystems for granted, but these resources rely on a cool climate, alkaline oceans and suitable habitats for biodiversity. If the chain in these ecosystems was suddenly broken or depleted, scientists predict their abundance will most certainly be affected.**

The disparity between natural ecosystems and consumerism in today's society is that big business and its dominance has killed off many small businesses which worked more closely within the laws of nature, while also being ecological for the community, such as the local butcher and family-run stores. The model of big business squeezes these smaller suppliers and businesses often out of existence, at a cost to our culture and global environment.

In the not so distant past the butcher would likely have been a family-run business, working closely with the farmer, so they **only supplied the needs of their customers**. Also they used the whole carcass (scarified animal), 'nose to tail' as it is known, instead of just the muscle areas. When a cat kills in the wild they will target a member of the herd that is older or weaker, mainly because catching an animal in its prime is dangerous to the cat's own health and survival, so the sacrifice is a balance with nature's lifecycles. After securing the kill, the cat will immediately eat the heart and liver because they are the most nutritious for its own survival.

The butcher followed these natural principles by remaining a small business, and only supplied what was in demand, whereas the supermarket chains are huge entities, **so big they need a supply chain spanning the globe. Cheap meat is paid for at the cost of the Earth's carbon footprint.** In doing so they supply more than they sell, therefore more waste is created than necessary, to provide the shopper with an unnatural level of convenience.

They also present their produce in uniform plastic casings, whereas the butcher hung their meat in a shop window and, on purchase, they wrapped the cuts in greaseproof paper as needed. A farmer told me that some years ago supermarkets would even inject red dye into their packaging to make the meat appear rich in blood.

Large corporations descend into our communities with the intention of taking most of the trade of smaller competition which cannot compete with the thrift on price they can offer. To illustrate this point about what small businesses are up against, I was chatting with a woman who had some party items in her hands. I said 'Did you go to a party shop?' and she replied, 'No way, it would cost a fortune, so I went to the pound shop', which was an equal distance away. When I asked her about it, she'd never been in the privately run party shop to check their prices, but her perception was that they would have been far more expensive.

Convenience for us is helping big businesses to squeeze their suppliers so that we save money in our pocket, but at what cost? Farmers with no say or bargaining power cannot compete with supermarket chains. They drive the farmers' prices down so that they can attract more customers in store and in doing so swallow up any competition and increase their profit margins, which are made on the back of the farming industry.

We the consumers need to take our share of responsibility, as we seek out discounted prices and are a very much becoming an 'I want it now culture', which is seen with the popularity of fast food delivery options in the last few years. Our perceived need for convenience makes us complicit in the perpetuation of the problem.

I'm using the supermarkets as an example but they are one of many, in a multitude of industries, eating up smaller businesses, a situation which is supported by the UK government. They are taking away the community spirit, with their faceless ownership and meaningless community boards and messages. They are creating enormous amounts of waste; small businesses would not otherwise do so.

Multinational corporations are detaching us from the natural environment that surrounds us. An example is the loss of **half** the Earth's rainforest within the last 100 years, cleared for their wood and land to farm for palm oil and beef cattle. In David Attenborough's book *A Life on Our Planet*, he reveals **the Amazon is on course to be reduced by 75% by the 2030s. The irony is that one Amazon is still growing, not in the real world of course, but on the internet. Is there a moral to this coincidence?**

By shrinking the rainforest the Earth loses habitats of biodiversity for half of all the known species in total, found nowhere else. World governments are powerless to stop these big businesses, or won't. No one is able to restrict them. I ask, is this convenience and an expectation of a standard of living really worth the amount of change and risk to our environment and our culture?

Stoic culture

I want to just take a moment to summarize what British and Irish culture means to me. It's a live-and-let-live attitude, filled with humour and empathy. Our humour is often sarcastic and self-deprecating but I wouldn't swap it for the world. Humour is how we build friendships and navigate through life with smiles on our faces. I myself come from a mixed nationality family as my mum is Irish and my dad is English. I lived in Scotland for many years when I was in the Marines and I met many Welsh people too. Like most people from our isles we are normally hard on the outside but soft on the inside.

People from the British and Irish isles are loyal, with a sense of fairness, and they can make light of the most serious and traumatic experiences, as an expression of healing and overcoming adversity. We generally support the underdog and will stand up to all types of cruelty and tyranny. We are difficult people to please, we moan when it's too cold and we moan when it's too hot, but our moaning isn't really moaning, its group therapy.

People might say that being stoic doesn't process emotions and people are just bottling them up. In the last chapter of the psychology section I will explain the difference between avoidance behaviour and being stoic. People can still practice stoicism and process their emotions. Stoicism is viewing all the evidence while holding your nerve, by not succumbing to fear in difficult situations. It's being guided by an internal moral compass of principles and values instead of reacting to fear.

Rudyard Kipling sums up stoicism in his poem 'If':

If you can keep your head when all about you
Are losing theirs and blaming it on you,
If you can trust yourself when all men doubt you,
But make allowance for their doubting too;

The stoic way

My parents are Baby Boomers and they are examples of stoicism. They were born in 1944 during the Second World War. They recall being toddlers in 1948 standing in line with their parents for rationing; food was scarce in comparison to today's abundance.

They had no amenities in their early years, which we take for granted today. There was no TV, microwave, fridge, dishwasher or washing machine; everything was cooked from scratch and cleaned by hand. They washed in a tub at home or at the swimming baths, which had a wash room with a bath tub. Their homes were heated by a fire but only in the room they were in or they lit one because someone wasn't well.

The highlight of my parents' childhoods was going to the picture house to watch the first TV on the big screen. They told me about cowboys and Indians, Charlie Chaplin, Laurel and Hardy. I asked how long they lasted and my mum said she wanted them to last forever because they were warm inside the picture house. They would think nothing of going outside and exploring to play from a young age.

While my siblings (four in total) and I were growing up, our family lived on my dad's single income, until we were old enough to attend school, at which point my mum took two jobs as a dinner lady and a cleaner. She decided after working in the school kitchen that she would take a college course to qualify as a school cook.

My dad worked on the railway all his life. Back then workers were loyal to their companies as they were to them. My dad had a job for life, as it was known. They were encouraged to socialize, exercise and were provided facilities to do so. The railway cared about my dad's wellbeing. He built lifelong work friendships with colleagues that he still keeps in touch with.

My parents worked hard inside and outside of the house and always put family first, and they made the best of the opportunities that came their way. Their own upbringing had taught them being a victim wasn't going to solve their problems. The wisdom of hardship cultivated a stoic mindset in them.

Living through rationing after the war made them frugal in nature from a young age; they wasted little, and even sour milk was used to make scones, or chicken bones would be saved to be used for soup. As working-class people, when buying they looked mostly for price. This didn't mean we received any less love; instead we learnt that the best things in life are free.

Back then bigger companies were the premium brands and

the small businesses were more cost effective. However this has shifted and now the opposite is true, as big business is not only interested in being a premium brand; they want more of the market share of the small businesses too. An example is when I was younger fruit and vegetable stores and markets were common – but how many fruit and vegetable shops or market traders do you see nowadays?

When I go back to my parents we frequent a large chain fast food restaurant for coffee. My parents go there many times a week, on the recommendation that the coffee is half the price of any competitor in the area. Big business exploits this predilection of my parents that was engrained into them growing up. It's not only my parents who frequent this large franchise, as this is easily the busiest business in that area, from all walks of life and age brackets.

I'm not absolutely against big business. There are certain industries like engineering that need significant investment for innovation. They are adding value to the modern world; however, I question how much value and innovation are added by conglomerate fast food chains and supermarkets, besides encouraging poor dietary habits, destroying small businesses and increasing our global carbon footprint. People say but they create jobs but the irony is so did smaller independent businesses without destroying our culture.

All I'm saying is instead of absolute support for big business I would like to see government focus on supporting smaller businesses too, as they are more than capable and they help retain our community spirit.

An example of how big business is warping our landscape, a large chain business went bust near our clinic and immediately the property was taken over by an insurance company. In the six months since opening, I could count on one hand the amount of customers I've seen enter their store. I'm guessing the cost of this store isn't coming from their store sales. A large organization like this can take on a lengthy lease without the individual store needing to turn a profit, keeping leases high, and this is why small business are disappearing.

It's not about becoming a holier than thou, virtue signaller, like the former Health Sectary of State, Matt Hancock who in 2020/21, even with the benefit of the doubt, acted as a misguided hypocrite. He abused his position of power, with a 'do as I say, not as I do' attitude. As I said I use big business on occasion, sometimes because of convenience, sometimes price and sometimes because it's the only choice. I am merely bringing awareness to a topic which I believe needs more balance; if there were scales for this they would be disproportionately tipped in favour of big business over small to medium-sized businesses.

Stoic values

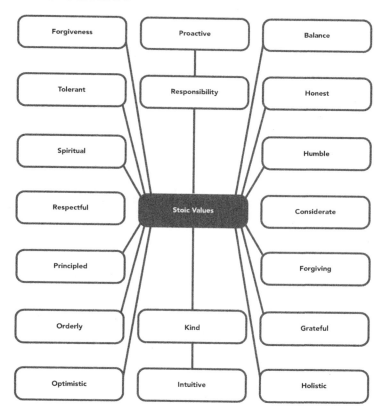

Albert Einstein

It's well known he struggled in the three R's system and therefore he self taught himself the sciences. He changed the way we thought about everything and even discovered how to time travel.

Nelson Mandela

Released from prison on Robin Island after 27 years in 1990, and then leading South Africa to end apartheid in 1996. His leadership was of forgiveness and unity.

Mohandas Gandhi

A remarkable rational and spiritual leader. A modern day prophet or saint in my opinion. Led India's struggles for independence with people power and peaceful disobedience.

Martin Luther King

Inspired by the teachings of Gandhi's peaceful disobedience, Martin Luther leads the civil rights movement. His speech "I have dream" is wise words for all time.

Examples of stoic people of the recent past

Muhammad Ali

Some say the greatest boxer of all time, not only for what he did in the ring but for what he did outside also. He never gave into fear or pressure to follow rules that he felt were unjust.

Abraham Lincoln

Led the union in the American civil war and he was instrumental in the epoch of freeing slaves. Big Ab never took any revenge on the confederate in victory.

Winston Churchill

Enigmatic Prime Minster and joint leader of the allies during world War Two, against the Nazi's. He was magnanimous in victory.

Florence Nightingale

She was the pioneer of the nursing profession during the Crimean War. She was known for her organization, leadership and holistic approach.

Benjamin Franklin

He was as significant as George Washington in the American Revolution before and after. All round good guy and liked by many in his time and he was an early defender of freedom of speech.

Mindset

Inside-out and outside-in mindset

The current system of society that supports big business encourages an **outside-in** mindset. When we perceive that an outside source is needed to complete us – a new phone, an asset, constant reassurance, friends and relationships – this is an outside-in mindset.

Business models exploit this mindset by creating needs that previously did not exist, then they create evidence and market reasons why you need their product. A need in the consumer is created, especially if their mindset is **outside-in** – 'If I just had this I would be happy'. In some cases consumers will depend on their product and even when the manufacturer 'makes to break' instead of making their product to last, they will be compelled to go out and get the latest upgrade.

We are being conditioned to think and act in a certain way, to suit their business models, and an **outside-in** mindset is more susceptible to these suggestions than an **inside-out** one. I understand this takes courage to step away from all we ever knew, the perceived comfort, success and achievement from living their way, but from my own experience I am much happier now by switching to an **inside-out** mindset.

The **inside-out** mindset is about being complete from the inside. I still use technology but technology doesn't complete me, I am complete already from the **inside out**. This means I spend more time in nature than on my phone, I read more books than I watch TV and when I watch TV I put the adverts on silent. If I need to make a decision, I make my decision from a set of values and principles that I've chosen, not by skilled marketing campaign. I question if my motives are made from fear and if so how I can overcome them and see beyond the fear to make a better decision.

I will go through some different mindsets over the next few pages and show their crossover. Our mindset controls our lives and will either give us power over our decisions or power to those suggesting things to us.

The military mindset

I'm privileged to be a member of the Union Jack Club in London, for serving and ex-serving servicemen and women. I connect with my past life as a serving member of the armed forces and socialize with other veterans. In the military, life is structured with discipline and teamwork, and in spite of discipline, humour is encouraged. I can instantly strike up friendship with most veterans because we share a similar history, hardships and a code of honour.

To encapsulate this mindset I would say this is a 'can-do' attitude, while also being eternally infected by a sense of humour. Here is an example of the last time I stayed. I was waiting in reception for breakfast to open and there were beer glasses from the night before, half finished in front of someone also waiting for breakfast. I said, deadpan with a nod towards the beer glasses, 'Are you starting early?' And he surprised me when he burst out laughing and exclaimed yes! And then I laughed too.

We struck up a conversation and had breakfast together, sharing stories of our experience of service and life in general. Throughout breakfast the conversation led to sensitive moments where we felt vulnerable but safe enough to drop our guard. That's my experience of veterans; I'm often surprised by their honesty and open sharing from the heart.

British servicemen and women are willing, courageous and self-reflective. Veterans I've met in civilian life are mostly successful in their new lives, not because of an arbitrary inclusion criterion but because they are hard-working, intelligent team members that others trust and see as role models. I know from speaking to many of them, they feel alienated from society, in an age where any comment or joke can be taken as offence.

A health inside-out mindset

The military mindset is associated with an inside-out approach. From my experience of being a practitioner, a patient with this mindset is motivated to regain their health when they become sick. They realize early on from the beginning what the triggers are, when they are identified to them. They believe they can get better and are willing to take responsibility for their situation. They can feel changes in their body and understand the value the practitioner is adding to their recovery. They are open to advice and trust the process that the practitioner has laid out for them.

They are generally bodily aware so once their triggers are identified they will avoid them. They understand the focus on a long-term strategy of healing, and how this takes time. They will be grateful to the practitioner for their help and support. They will question and want to understand how treatment works and how they can help themselves in future.

They understand the body has its own intelligence and are prepared to surrender to that intelligence to heal. They realize that pain medication is only masking the symptoms and will want to resolve the cause instead.

A health outside-in mindset

The opposite mindset to inside-out is outside-in. This mindset is always looking for an outside source to complete them, such as an instant fix pill or procedure.

In my experience as a practitioner this sort of patient will need constant reassurance that the problem can be resolved, even after multiple explanations and signs of recovery. They question regularly whether this is working for them and will likely drop off of care when their pain has resolved. They lack the ability to go inside and feel their own body, and feel the changes that are being made.

They are more likely to continue the trigger that is the cause of the problem, delaying the healing process. When this happens they will blame anyone else without consideration. They are reactive only, without foresight or reflection.

They do not take responsibility for their current situation and they make short-term choices or quick-fix decisions, risking a recurrence of the problem or causing further complications and compensations. They are impatient, only focused on relieving their pain and not interested in a long-term strategy. They usually are conditioned to believe health comes from the outside, such as from a pill, and therefore do not believe that they can help themselves.

Ask yourself this question: which mindset will speed up the healing process? If a person takes more than a moment's consideration or they are still considering now, they more than likely have an outside-in mindset with regard to health. If a person's internal dialogue is struggling to connect (their beliefs are connected to their healing time and quality), they might want to address this with themselves, especially if they want long-term best results and to limit recurrence of injury. Those that know the answers quickly are more than likely of an inside-out mindset.

The fear mindset

An outside-in mindset is associated with the fear mindset. There is an old adage: sticks and stones may break my bones but words will never hurt me. The fear mindset is offended by any comment, even if those comments are educational and constructive. This mindset is encapsulated by an attitude of 'why me?' (notice the difference to 'can do') and they will seek blame and shift responsibility away from themselves onto others as a resolution.

This focus on blame without self-reflection is self-interested or shares the limited interests of a subset group, like those of fanatical religions. Blame has the appearance of resolving issues and individuals may feel better knowing that someone else is at fault, but it is more associated with the teaching of 'an eye for eye' instead of Jesus's teaching of forgiveness by turning the other cheek.

This mindset focuses on the past to seek revenge and retribution retrospectively instead of learning what the lessons of the past are. People with this mindset want to censor freedom of speech and freedom of the press and will campaign against anyone with a different opinion to them. They will trawl through comments of living people to condemn them, creating a society where everyone has to look over their shoulder.

Our leaders after the Second World War set up many of the systems so that we can currently live in peace today. A contrasting style to these systems of peace is Stalin's Russia, where people with the slightest indifference to the state had their houses raided at night by secret police and were never seen again. It was well known that after Stalin had given a speech the crowd clapped continuously because they were warned the first person to stop clapping would be shot. We can control with fear and coercion, but it's not the enlightened way and has been shown to slow innovation, economic growth and quality of life.

In my opinion, we are an enlightened nation, backed by history, standing up to tyrants like Napoleon and Hitler. The Emperor, as Napoleon liked to be known, had invaded and plundered most countries in Europe over a twenty-year period and was only defeated by a joint European effort. Napoleon and Hitler had striking similarities in their intentions and on both occasions we stood up against them. They were only opposed initially by the people of the British Isles and their bulldog spirit.

To people quick to question our enlightened attitude, I say imagine either of these bullyies had had their way and conquered Europe – would there be less discrimination in the world?

They were megalomaniacs set on creating new empires and world domination, as if they were playing the board game Risk. Hitler had ordered books in libraries to be burnt so as to control the knowledge of the people. After Napoleon's defeat and capture, instead of facing the guillotine like so many others had under his orders in the French Revolution, he was shown mercy and exiled in the custody of the British Navy twice.

Napoleon is famous for moaning about his treatment in letters on St Helena, where he stayed for the remainder of his life after the conclusion of the Napoleonic wars. Had I been on sunny St Helena I would have been glad I still had my head, but then is that just my Britishness showing, always wanting to make the best of a bad situation.

Many countries are still part of the Commonwealth and they

retain the Union Jack (a flag with a combination of crosses of St George, St Andrew and St Patrick) in one quadrant, representing our shared values, common goal and heritage.

Genius mindset

The UK was the first for many inventions, reforms and freedoms that we and other first world counties take for granted today.

We were the first to set up a modern democratic governmental system, which began the process, in time, of universal suffrage to all adults. Althoughor 600 years or more our parliament only allowed the vote to nobles, gentry, lawyers and moneyed merchants; even into the 19th century, approximately only one person in a hundred had a vote. I might add this was the same throughout the world at the time and our parliament was the first to take steps to a majority rule. We were the first to set up labour laws, protection for tenants against exploiting landlords, and provide organized and free education for children and set a working age limit for them and their working hours.

We outlawed capital punishment for any crime in 1968 and banned trading slaves in the Commonwealth by 1809, long before any other nation. In the UK we never lived under segregation or apartheid – quite the opposite, people of all creeds, races and religions are accommodated and encouraged to live by their cultures in the United Kingdom. The working-class people of this country supported India's struggle for independence led by Gandhi's genius of peaceful protest; they also supported Lincoln's union during the American Civil War.

After the Second World War we set revolutionary ideas in motion: the National Health Service, investment in schooling and a welfare system, to allow equal opportunity for all and to stop those who are old, sick or disabled from falling below the poverty line. These are seen today as essential standards of any first world government country today and they started here.

Most of the technology we take for granted in the 21st centuries, like the advent of computers and smartphones, exists because of a magic period of innovation during the 19th century. After the Napoleonic wars ended the industrial revolution saw the rise of steam (pun intended), and the building of railways throughout the Commonwealth which are still in use today. The telephone, harnessing electricity, refrigeration, the flushing toilet, the first sewers and underground railways were all invented and discovered by the genius minds of their time in this archipelago of the British and Irish isles.

A Japanese study showed that 54% of the entire world's useful inventions of the last 100 years were discovered in the UK and originate from this period of our history. That's half the world's inventions with 1% of the world population. We also boast more Nobel Prize winners than any other nation apart from the United States, but their population is over four times the UK's.

Magna Carta

I believe this was all made possible by the epoch of the Magna Carta, which paved the way for establishing a set of laws to give individuals basic freedoms, which was the template for the American Declaration of Independence, the Bill of Rights and constitutional amendments as newer iterations.

Very shortly after Magna Carta was signed a new age began; the first university colleges were built in Oxford and Cambridge which are today in the top ten universities in the world and are prestigious institutions (today most cities have a university). Nothing had been seen of the like in education settings since the great Greek civilization. This was also the beginning of a structured and traditional path to allow people from all backgrounds social mobility through education. Again this all started here.

Freedom to be a genius

Under these freedoms a genius mindset would flourish to produce world-famous writers such as William Shakespeare, Charles Dickens, Mary Shelley and Arthur Conan Doyle, and scientists such as Roger Bacon, Francis Bacon, William Harvey, Michael Faraday, William Gilbert, Isaac Newton, George Stevenson, James Watt, Lord Kelvin, Charles Darwin, John Dalton Alex Bell, Alexander Fleming and Sir Tim Berners-Lee.

Sea heroes like Horatio Nelson, Francis Drake, Walter Raleigh,

Collingwood, Cornwallis, St Vincent and James Cook. Great thinkers and polymaths such as Alan Watts, Bertrand Russell, Benjamin Franklin (born in America to English parents but he also spent 20 odd years in the UK – an honorary Brit in my opinion) and Rupert Sheldrake. Pioneers of architecture and engineering such as John Vanbrugh, Christopher Wren and Isambard Kingdom Brunel.

We weren't bad at comedy either: Charlie Chaplin, one half of Laurel and Hardy, Monty Python, the two Ronnies, Morecambe and Wise, Ben Elton, Mr Bean and *Only Fools and Horses*. Other legends include Florence Nightingale, Winston Churchill, The Beatles, and One Direction (OK the last one is debatable). These are the minds that inspire us.

We are all potential geniuses

The genius mindset applies to someone who can maintain an open mind, gather information, see beyond conventional thinking and draw their own conclusions. As the times evolve so must our thinking. In doing so we imagine new and improved products, services or systems which were not possible to conceive from conventional thinking.

This mindset suits a system and government that supports higher-minded philosophy, and encourages people to think instead of thinking for them. When people are fearful they think less for themselves and need more guidance from an outside source and as a consequence we produce fewer people with a genius mindset. The fear and genius mindset are opposites of one another. Everyone has the potential to be a genius and more people will fulfil their potential if we can overcome the fear mindset.

I invite you to find your genius. Before going any further what went through your mind when you read my invite, were you filled with fear or were you filled with possibility? These thoughts and feelings are a guide to your current mindset. The genius mindset is linked to the **inside-out** mindset, and the fear mindset is linked to the **outside-in** one. When we feel fear we do not think straight, we lose control of reality and our senses and therefore are more inclined to look outside of the self for answers.

Mindset

Inside out	Outside in
Ability to think like a genius	Limited thinking due to fear
Empowered	Victim
Taking responsibility	Blame others
Can do attitude	Why me attitude
Encourage freedoms	Limit freedoms
Long term focus	Short term fixes

I am not saying that every veteran I meet is of higher-minded principles and that they represent my worldview, or that they would make good leaders, but I know they can follow leaders because they were led by British officers in the services, who in my experience were intelligent, moral and had a strong sense of fairness and responsibility. Veterans are always polite and well mannered to strangers and I've always found them to be wise, knowledgeable and pragmatic.

We must focus on the present and make that present equal for all, while rewarding merit and honesty. Being British isn't about a bloodline or where you are born; it's about being free to live a set of stoic principles and values and prepared to defend those freedoms regardless of the odds.

I propose a new nationalism but instead of a national pride, a collective nationalism of thinking bigger than ourselves by creating a sustainable future for us and future generations globally. As previously mentioned we led the world before with our evolving genius mindset and this is needed more than ever now.

Our ancestors harnessed great innovations from the environment without knowing the true cost. Today those environmental concerns are plain to see and we must put these costs before profit. Already geniuses propose a plan, a circular environmental economy of no pollution, renewable energy captured by the Sun, with no plastics and where what we do use is reusable and biodegradable; all that is needed is to spread the word gently to others and reconnect with the old attitudes of the past that served my parents so well.

Healthy mindset

Health and mindset are one and the same. A stoic mindset of taking responsibility for your health and being positive uses the power of the placebo effect, meaning we are more likely to be healthy because we believe ourselves to be so. When we focus on a victim mindset we are prone to blame others and not take responsibility for our health. This is called the nocebo effect, which is the opposite of the placebo effect, meaning we are more likely to become sick and unhealthy because of our mindset.

Our health is more valuable to us than all the money in the world and is a blessing from the universe but health is not a thing or person, health is a collection of cells, systems and organs working together. Health is the holistic cooperation of life, to grow and die, so that we can renew into the next generation.

In summary

As I said in the beginning I'm not inventing a new philosophy; most of Stoical Beingism is taken from other people's work, pieced together to make a modern, relevant philosophy for the here and now, for the needs of our own health and the needs of our planet. For example, live and let live is an old saying that our ancestors lived by, treating all beings as equals is a precept in Buddhism and expressing gratitude is what people do when they pray. The saying that someone is always worse off than you is a favourite saying of parents everywhere.

All I want to do is reclaim the meaning of these eternal wisdoms, swallowed up by the rational enlightenment and digital age, and regurgitate them back into existence. The usual argument against philosophy to find a solution for the world's problems is that philosophy isn't pragmatic, but I hope this chapter has shown that philosophy is not only capable of being pragmatic but is also vital to our survival.

My goal by presenting this chapter in this book is that people will start to think about philosophy again when deciding how they live their lives. Then like me I hope they develop their own philosophy that makes sense to them.

Let us pray

An alternative non secular prayer to finish the mass:

Let us give thanks and praise to the Universal Power,

We are gifted this life on earth and regardless of the reason we are in eternal gratitude,

We trust this Universal POWER to guide us on our PATH,

We wish all universal beings and non-beings peace, joy and happiness.

Philosophy quiz

1) What is a philosophy?

a) Inferior to science

b) Useless and meaningless

c) Logic that can be disproved

d) Logic that cannot be disproved

2) The saying 'someone is always worse off than you' is said by who?

a) The fairy godmother

b) Parents everywhere

c) First world countries

d) Matt Hancock

3) A law of nature is?

a) Growth and entropy

b) Asset stripping

c) Immortal life

d) Uncooperative

4) Which of those laws is scientifically proven to help you be happier, healthier and live longer?

5) The universe is?

a) A static shape

b) Expanding in all direction

c) Centred around earth

d) Is finite

6) Stoical Beingism values?

a) Seeking revenge

b) Choosing to be a victim

c) Tolerance

d) Supports greenwashing

7) Health is?
a) Only understood by medical professionals
b) Something to fix only when broken
c) Only about your own individual health
d) A collective of an internal and external environment

8) A circular economy means?
a) Gaining profit and power in the market
b) A throwaway culture
c) A reusable society
d) Encouraging the use of virgin plastics

9) In the last 60 years the Amazon rainforest will be reduced by what percentage by the 2030s?
a) 75%
b) Will only exist on the internet
c) 50%
d) 25%

10) An inside-out mindset means someone?
a) Believes health comes from a external source
b) Need constant reassurance
c) Focuses on short-term fixes
d) Takes responsibility for their health

11) An outside-in mindset means someone?
a) Believes health comes from an external source
b) Focuses on long-term strategy
c) Thinks for themselves
d) Draws their own conclusions

Microbiology and smaller

Physics, big and small

The atom

At the tiniest level of our understanding of matter is the atom, standing at one ten-millionth of a millimetre to be exact. When we think of the atom we tend to think of quantum physics, the newly discovered science in the 20th century, which is mysterious and counterintuitive. The great patron saint of science Albert Einstein was boggled by quantum physics' randomness. Although the origins of the word atom date back to the Greek word, meaning 'a little mass', so small that it cannot be separated. Somehow without a Large Hadron Collider, the Greeks deduced, from their genius mindset, that matter is smaller than the eye can see and can be broken down into tiny atoms.

The atom is made up of three parts, the nucleus, which is compacted with positively charged protons and then surrounded by a force field of electrons that are negatively charged. The third part is neutrons and they are neither negatively nor positively charged but they add mass to the atom. The atom is mostly empty space with little density, as the nucleus is where most of the density is found. To give you an idea of the size to weight ratio between the two, if the electron field was the size and height of London's tallest building, the Shard, the positively charged nucleus would be the size of a fly. However the fly would be thousands of times heavier than the building.

These tiny particles combine together to make molecules, to form not only us but everything in the universe. They are the underlying matrix that connects all things and all beings, which are by far the most abundant thing in the universe, in numbers that might as well be infinite to us. Quantum physics is so mysterious that we needed to design a whole new set of laws and principles to accommodate the small world into our understanding of Newtonian and Einstein physics.

The paradox of gravity

In the macro-level world, gravity shapes orbits of smaller planets or stars around a larger gravitational pull such a super massive black hole. Einstein's theory of relativity showed that we orbit around the gravitational pull of the sun in a three-dimensional universe. Imagine a bowling ball on a mattress; the heavier the bowling ball is the more the ball would sink into the mattress. Now imagine marbles scattered on the mattress – the closer they are to the depressed area from the bowling ball, the more it will pull them towards the mass in the centre.

How far the bowling ball sinks into the mattress represents a gravitational pull and the bowling ball represents a large object in space, causing a gravitational force. Since Newtonian and Einstein physics, gravity has snugly fitted the macro world into an order of time, space and gravitation forces; however in the micro-level world of the small, at the level of the atom, there is no gravitational force or time, just space, lots and lots of space.

The electron jigsaw (neither here nor there)

Atoms fit together with other atoms that complement each other, making molecules by combining and connecting to other atoms' electromagnetic fields. They fit together like jigsaw pieces by sharing electrons within each other's fields, forming a bond. In the normal world of physics, A to B is essentially moving one object to another over a time period, just like when we travel in a car to visit a destination. It is expressed by the equation mass x distance = time/speed.

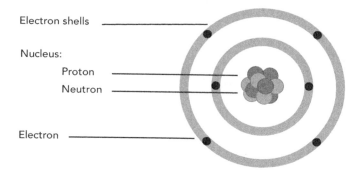

Electron shells

Nucleus:

Proton

Neutron

Electron

However, at the atomic level electrons can appear and then reappear immediately in another position without travelling across the space in-between, known as the quantum leap. (There was a great TV show of that name, if you're old enough to remember.) It's similar to *Star Trek* when Scotty beams up members of the crew to go from one place instantly to another. It's impossible in Newtonian and Einstein physics to change position without physically travelling the distance, but at the quantum level this is possible. Electrons are nowhere and everywhere all at the same time, without following linear orbits like the planets in our solar system.

Studies of subatomic particles show that they can be separated and scientists observe, somehow no matter what the distance, that they are able to communicate with one another by instantly mirroring in reaction to the connected particle, faster than the speed of light. This discovery breaks Einstein's theory of relativity law, which stated nothing can travel faster than the speed of light, but here was evidence to contrary. Like so much of the atom and its counterintuitive ways, we are only able to observe this, without an explanation as to how it happens.

The atom is terribly self-conscious, as when the electron

field is being observed it reacts differently to when it's not. A dual personality if you like, behaving as a particle when observed, but changing to behave as a wave when no one's looking; therefore predicting electrons is impossible. Whereas in macro physics we can predict the orbit of Earth because there is no duality. When we look at the other planets in the solar system we can predict their orbits many years in advance because they follow a definitive path around the Sun.

Imagine if the solar system suddenly became part of the quantum world, Earth would not only appear in its current orbit, but would appear in any possible orbit around the Sun, being everywhere and nowhere all at the same, only existing when being observed and everywhere else the rest of the time. There would no definitive linear orbits to predict, planets would be able to time travel instantly to any areas of the solar system. Now we know how Doctor Who does it.

In a heated inflationary universe like the one in which we exist, everything that has a beginning has an end. Everything in existence grows, matures and then begins to decay, apart from the atom. Atoms again escape the known laws of the universe and seemingly can last forever, continuing to shape and change into other objects over time.

Scratching your head? Don't worry, you're not the only one – so are the greatest living minds of quantum physicists. So much so that there's a saying amongst quantum physicists, 'If a person says they understand quantum physics, they misunderstood what was being said.' In my experience, these scientists tend to be more open minded and spiritual than other area of science, perhaps because of the complexity of the subject that refuses to be neatly explained, like other branches of science. The best that can say of this is that keeping an open mind is the most prudent approach when discussing the quantum arena.

Microbiology

Like quantum physics, microbiology is a fairly new branch of science and was made possible by the invention of the microscope. Originally called cell theory in the Victorian era, this has developed into modern microbiology. With the increased magnification of microscopes, our understanding of cells and bacteria has become greater. We have now been opened up to an intricate and cooperative, webbed water world. In each cell thousands of chemical reactions happen in sequence every second to support our life force and for our survival.

Homeostasis (the economy of the body)

At a molecular level the membrane (outside wall of the cell) is the communication centre, constantly monitoring the internal and external environment. When the membrane receives information, instructions are sent to maintain what's called homeostasis. An internal consciousness beyond our control is always gauging the environment for the health and survival of our cells. They will adjust, change and correct within their control to stay with these parameters that are compatible with homeostasis.

It is similar to a society where people work for a common good and contribute through taxes towards a gross domestic product so that an office worker in an inner city can rely on household and public amenities such as food, water and fuel to be supplied by other industries. The shared roles of society and industry allow people doing specific roles to be able to function and for their work to complement each other just in the same way the cells do. Think of homeostasis as an internal economy or order of distribution of resources. Specific cells and bacteria perform a role and are fed and nurtured by resources with a priority to maintain inner harmony of our internal environment.

Health is measured by our body's ability to maintain homeostasis, the stable internal environment needed for our cells to flourish. These messages from our cells are communicated through the nervous system that order other systems to release or suppress a chemical, such as hormones or enzymes, to restore balance. Our body's ability to regulate homeostasis is closely related to what we eat, how much or little we exercise, how we handle stress and our beliefs and the subsequent emotions they cause.

Imagine someone is run down by stress, so they take some time off to rest; they feel better in a few days, as their body can go through an innate healing process utilizing our immune system to flush out toxins, returning the body to homeostasis. We heal best when we remove triggers that are stressful and potential causes.

Imagine if they decided to not rest: over time they risk exhaustion, forcing them into rest. Our body will only work responsively for a short period outside of homeostatic ranges before signs and symptoms will arise or we are forced to stop. Many diseases are preventable by understanding these bodily processes, of spotting the signs and symptoms in their early stages of disease.

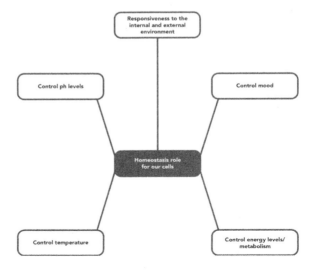

Bacteria

A bacterium is so small it cannot be seen with the naked eye; even with lab microscopes they are difficult to spot, but they are there, in abundance everywhere and essential to all life. These microbes form 80% of all organic living matter on Earth. The other 20% is plants, animals and fungi. We are included in the animals and although bigger, we are a small minority compared to essential microbes.

Bacteria live inside all of us, they are as vital to our life force and survival as food and water is; this might surprise many, but this is certainly the case. We could not live without them, but bacteria could live without us.

Their presence is ubiquitous to human life, by living on our skin, mouths and digestive tracts, performing vital and essential tasks. They are much smaller than human cells but are far more numerous. Every human is home to 10 quadrillion bacterial cells; in our digestive tract alone, we are home to 100 trillion microbes of various types. We depend on bacteria to break down food further than the digestive system is able to do. They help us absorb vitamins and minerals, and they convert food sources into energy that otherwise the body couldn't do alone.

Think of bacteria like a regenerating machine, capable of digesting an element, to rearrange this element into something else. When we are alive this chemistry set maintains life in harmony. When we die, bacteria acts as the universal caretaker, recycling our bodies back into the universe. Bacteria serve us well while we are alive and afterwards will help return us back to the cosmos.

This is the miracle of life. If bacteria did not exist nothing organic would be able to rot, and nothing in life would be able to regenerate once those cells died. We were never meant to last forever; life is time limited and for good reason, so that the next generation can live on in our place. Bacteria started this chain of events of passing on genetic code at the deep sea vents approximately 3.5 billions of years ago. We need to thank bacteria for playing their role in being the ancestors to everyone.

They are also important to maintaining the atmosphere

with oxygen. Algae and bacteria fill the atmosphere with oxygen through photosynthesis. These tiny organisms produce 150 billion kilograms of oxygen every year. Other notable achievements of bacteria are that they help to regenerate depleted soil, they purify water and they help our immune systems fight foreign invaders when they enter our body. It seems that bacteria do more for us than we realize, so why do they get such a bad rep?

They are probably the most misunderstood aspect of modern science. Bacteria on the whole are friendly to us – only one bacterium in a thousand is a pathogen. Also a lot depends on the current health of the person who contracts the pathogen, whether they become sick or not. Bacteria support immune functions by fighting other bacterial pathogens that enter the body; they are generally more friend than foe. If bacteria are going to make ha ome inside of us then the last thing they want to do is kill their host.

The cell

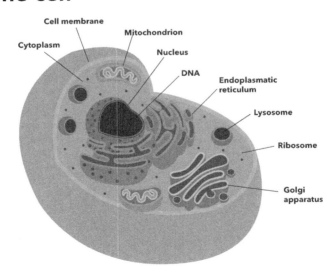

At a 200th of a millimetre our cells are much bigger than bacteria and atoms but they are still tiny, only observable under a microscope. A thousand chemical reactions are happening every second within the cell and outside is a marketplace for cells and bacteria to live side by side in a cooperative of trading and bartering in our internal environment. The main difference between a cell and bacteria is that our cells use oxygen as an energy source while most bacteria are anaerobic, which means they use alternative fuel sources and will avoid oxygen.

Complex life is possible because a billion years ago a new type of cell evolved, called the eukaryote cell. They were much bigger than any bacteria and so they incorporated bacteria within the structure. Imagine an underwater city metropolis of nearly 10,000 individual moving parts. Then at some point in the past these cells made the jump from unicellular organisms to being part of a multicellular organism, which would lead to us.

We are approximately 60-100 trillion eukaryote cells, combining to make a whole human being. We are made up of many types of cells and their function varies. Red blood cells bind to oxygen and carbon dioxide, nerve cells send and receive electrical signals, muscle cells slide over one another for flexibility or to generate force and lastly bone cells allow a strong but pliable frame. Each cell's function and structure will depend on what their role in life is and the health of the cells that surround them. As we will find out, cells depend on one another, just as we depend on them.

Mini me

The cell is like a tiny human in the sense they consist of small organs called organelles. They consist of their own skeleton, which is called a cytoskeleton; this maintains the shape of a cell, much like our bones do. There is a nucleus for producing proteins and an outer skin, called a membrane.

A mitochondrion is a sort of bacteria that lives inside the cell, but one of the few bacteria that uses oxygen as a fuel source. Known as the power house of the cell, oxygen is converted into electrical energy for the cell to function. The mitochondrion has DNA separate to our cells and could live outside of the cell. At some point in the past mitochondria took up residence within the cell as mutual business partners if you like. They are a cautious business partner, though, as they will only pass down the generations through females.

The cell membrane

The cell membrane is a sturdy but flexible structure. Imagine a balloon filled with water; it would be squidgy to touch but the outer surface would retain the water inside. This is what the membrane of the cell does, acting as a pliable outer wall to hold in the cell's contents. Its job is to maintain the internal environment of the cell, whilst also monitoring the external environment for signals and communicating with other cells. It has many antennas on the surface, acting as satellites, sending and receiving messages from other cells and the external environment.

To get into the cell you need accreditation. By this I mean if you're not useful to the cell, such as protein, fats, oxygen, hormones or enzymes, the likelihood of getting in is slim. If there's no receptor to bind onto when entering a gateway, they will not open; however, if the receptor binds to a molecule, an electrical charge will open the gateway.

This makes the membrane wall a fortress, protecting and separating the internal contents of the cell from the outside environment. Water is one of the few substances that can pass through the outer wall freely, known as osmosis. This is when water goes from high concentration to a low concentration. Imagine a lock on a barge of a canal being opened and water falling under the weight of gravity into shallower waters.

Between the walls is a fatty layer, which repels water, so water doesn't stay there for long. When hot fat is mixed with water and cools, the fat will rise above the water into two layers; for the reason mentioned, fat and water do not mix in their chemical structure. The cell uses chemistry to control its environment.

Inside and outside water

The water inside the cell is called intercellular water. The cycle for intercellular water to be replenished is about four to six weeks, making up two thirds of total fluid in our body. The cell is like a fish tank that self-replenishes, so that the water inside doesn't become stagnant. Most of the water in our cells is in a solution, which means that gas and other useful materials, such as nutrients and enzymes (chemical compounds for speeding up chemical reactions) are dissolved. This mix of gas and chemicals is the opposite of the fatty layer within the membrane wall, in the sense that it attracts instead of repels water.

Extracellular fluid is in the spaces between cells. The concentration of the solution inside and outside the cell will be different, depending on what the cell needs at that time to function and what is available in the extracellular fluid. When deliveries are made from the outside to the inside, the concentration of solution inside the cell will break down nutrients out of their packaging for metabolizing and use this as energy. Once the cell has used what it needs it will recycle the contents back into the outside fluid.

This process is the cell's digestive system. When we think of a digestive system we might think of teeth or swallowing but the cell is one the oldest living systems on the planet. This means our cells digest for energy, growth and repair. They also protect themselves from disease through internal immune cells that will engulf and destroy bacteria or foreign substances entering the cell.

DNA

Inside the nucleus is the library of ourselves – this is where our DNA is stored. These are the blueprints; every piece of matter that ever produced us started here. If for example a protein is needed, the DNA library is opened but no books ever leave; instead a copy is made known as RNA. This is a copy of the plans of how to build proteins, the building blocks of life.

Due to discoveries in epigenetics we now know that the membrane of the cell is the brain and the nucleus is like the reproductive organs. Genes are activated by the environment of the cell, sensed by the membrane and are not absolutely self-determined by our genetic family history.

Through this understanding of epigenetics, science is teaching us we can harness more power over our health than previously believed. In days gone by we were told to believe that because our grandparents had a certain cancer or heart disease, we were destined to follow the same fate. It is not so. Although there are genetic disorders that are passed on, there is no gene activated at birth for cancer or for heart disease. These develop over a lifetime and are more likely to be as a result of stress management issues, lifestyle factors or inherited behaviours.

Therefore our genes do not control our destiny – instead our beliefs, emotions and environment do.

Evolution is epigenetic

Epigenetics is the branch of science championed by Bruce Lipton, and which discovered the membrane of the cell is coordinating the communication within and outside of the cell. If there is a change in the external environment, the cell membrane orders the cells to alter and change chemical reactions to the needs of the body, working individually and collectively. The nucleus of the cell is not predetermined and acts in accordance with instructions from the membrane, which is monitoring changes in the external environment.

When Charles Darwin formulated his theory of evolution after visiting the Galapagos Islands, he based his theory on recognizing the difference between similar species adapted to take advantage of these isolated environments. Different species of finches, for example, had specially adapted, longer beaks to peck between the crevices of rocks, than fiches on other islands that pecked from flat ground. For me this is an example of the cell membrane adjusting our make up to take advantage of our environment.

To give a real world analogy of the crossover between evolution theory and epigenetic processes, imagine an American football game. The object of the game is to gain ground against an opponent that is defending and also wants to gain ground towards the end zone where points are scored. Plays are executed by the quarterback (conscious consciousness). On the sideline the coach (cell membrane) chooses the oncoming players to best suit the quarterbacks' needs. When the ball is played, the quarterback throws the ball to his teammate, in space to exploit the other team's defensive weaknesses (in nature, other species of plants and animals).

Adventurous evolutionary changes in the external environment are connected to the internal environment via the signals received by the cell membrane.

Another analogy is golf. A good golfer will be able to judge distance and then pick the best club for the distance. Imagine the club in the golfer's mind's eye is custom made for each shot. The clubs are produced by the interpretation of the cell membrane of the golfer's consciousness, therefore ordering the nucleus to produce the correct length of the club based on the consciousness of the golfer. The more accurate the clubs the nucleus can produce, the more chance the golfer will outperform other golfers. The nucleus is using information from the cell membrane to determine evolutionary adaptation.

The innate consciousness of microbiology

A novel idea I would like to present here is this: what if consciousness isn't in the brain as previously thought by modern science? There has been extensive study into the anatomy and function of the brain on MRI scans, yielding interesting discoveries, but no study has been able to find a thought or a feeling, only the areas of the brain sensing them. The brain is the nerve centre but what if the brain isn't controlling self-determining thought or feeling?

What if the brain is only showing the sensations of consciousness and instead consciousness is somewhere else? Philosophers as far back as the Greeks and early Buddhists asked these questions; some even suggested consciousness is outside of the self. For all the research that I've seen, it's only reinforced my belief that consciousness isn't in the brain at all. The brain is a marvellous computer in itself but no evidence can be found that consciousness is central there or that the brain itself has directed consciousness.

My own hypothesis is that consciousness is in the cells and possibly also bacteria, and the combined organization of all the cells results in 'conscious consciousness'. We know that cells and bacteria are controlling parts of our subconscious – they control our mood, so is it too far a stretch in imagination to consider that

89

they may form part of the consciousness that we identify with as being 'us'?

In the not so distant past, cells and bacteria were independent living parts, separate from one another. It seems logical to me that they would consist of conscious and subconscious parts if they were to survive on their own. There is substantial evidence that plants display consciousness and they are without brains or nervous systems, but they do share similar cell biology to us.

The closest philosophies that I have found to this are panentheism and animism; the former goes one step further by saying that consciousness is in the atom and molecule, which is also plausible. Whereas animism is an older logic, before the rational Enlightenment, when people believed everything is somehow connected.

The main difference between atoms, cells and bacteria is that the latter two need to digest energy to survive. As far as we know atoms and molecules can exist indefinitely if undisturbed without a fuel source, whereas bacteria and cells need to search for food sources, adding a degree of complexity to their survival, which atoms and molecules do not need.

Originally, consciousness in its most basic form might be the hunger at the molecular level, and over time those simpler cellular structures combined to form more complex, self-organizing structures, meaning a combined consciousness, with the intention to find fuel sources for individual cells and bacteria. Our nervous system is newer on the evolutionary chain and the general belief is that consciousness developed from there – but are we to say that there was no consciousness before this point in time?

It makes sense to me that nature is not only alive but is also conscious to some degree, in the same way that animals with nervous systems are conscious too. We know that trees can communicate with one another through the fungal network in their root systems, but they are without nervous systems.

For most mammals life begins as a single cell; in humans, this is called a sperm. Through the act of conception sperm are released to find their way to an awaiting egg to be fertilized. In the egg the sperm will divide many times to form a foetus. Cells will continue to divide throughout a lifetime. We were all once a single sperm, intelligent enough to find its way to a fertile egg. It makes sense to me our consciousness began long before we are born.

Once we accept that the cell is intelligent we can then start to explore this idea I've presented. I would like to see someone prove me wrong on this but looking in the brain for the answer is in the wrong place.

Other microbiological responses

We are now going to discuss responses in the body which are the on the cusp of starting the next chapter, Biology, viewing them within systems of the body. I will be discussing these microbiological parts as individual components before discussing them as part of a greater system. These homeostatic responses are the purpose of the system.

Blood (the carrier of responses)

The blood is made up of red and white blood cells, plasma and platelets. Let's look at them individually. Red blood cells (RBCs) are by far the biggest component of blood – 25 billion are in a teaspoon. They are a specialist cells with an affinity (a chemical word for fitting together) for oxygen and carbon dioxide.

Blood doping in sport is when an athlete injects RBCs into their bloodstream so there are more oxygen carriers to cells improving endurance. This performance-enhancing procedure is banned, but is also very dangerous because when RBCs are added, the blood becomes less watery and thicker, which runs the risks of blood clots.

That's where plasma is useful because it's mostly water and is full of antibodies, which help with the clotting process if we get a cut for instance. RBCs and blood plasma make up the bulk of blood and are joined by white blood cells (WBCs), which make up 1%; and platelets also account for 1%. WBCs are like sentries that monitor the blood for any pathogens and will answer a distress call from any cell in the body, with response time in minutes.

There are approximately six to eight pints of blood in a normal adult, which as mentioned mainly consists of red blood cells and plasma. The RBCs renew every four months before being recycled by the liver as an aid to digestion. It's not known if the remaining red blood cells gather for a wake but if they did, this is what the high priest of red blood cells might say:

Obituary of a red blood cell

We are gathered here today to the resting place of Red, second name Cell, who many of us knew. During their life they were a tireless worker, combining work with travel. They made over 100,000 circles through the circulatory system, in a vascular system they called home. In that time they travelled approximately 100 miles in total. When they retired from the circulatory service, they relocated to the liver, doing charity work for the Bilirubin Foundation. They will not be forgotten and forever remembered (bilirubin makes our bowel movements brown).

A day in the life of a red blood cell
Picks up oxygen in the lungs /depot in the lungs pick up goods
They take the fastest route via the heart superhighway (Arteries)
Is under pressure but always delivers (blood pressure)
Arrives at cell in timely fashion
Even get rid of the rubbish (carbon dioxide)
Keeps our organs and muscles working, sometime overtime depending on how busy everyone is
Picks rations up from the liver and digestive tract
Whatever fluid is lost travels back thru the lymph network
At some point they take a shower in the kidney after a hard day's work

White blood cells (immune response)

The immune system is like the emergency services and the Navy rolled into one. They run a tight ship. They know us and they know what's not. Let's just say we went for a stroll in disguise at cellular level and the immune system identified us as not being us; that's your cue to drop the disguise because they are commissioned to remove unidentified objects by whatever means necessary.

WBCs circulate the blood identifying any potential invaders. If any part of us is considered not us, then those initial WBCs are a reconnaissance group for the immune system. They will watch the invader's movements, profiling them, cross-referencing them with anything that has been seen before, weighing and sizing them up. This information is passed back through the chain of command and an appropriate taskforce is assembled for the inevitable battle that will ensue.

Once the taskforce is ready the WBCs will surround and engulf the foreign body and usually destroy anything they capture. If the pathogen is recognized by the immune system then sometimes all that is needed is the release of antibodies, which sweep up the pathogen without full on war. This is called memory immunity and means that the cells and microbes are wise to the pathogen and can handle the situation diplomatically on repeat occasions.

Sometimes the pathogen isn't an invader at all, but is instead a threat from within, like a rogue cancerous cell. The cell has become unresponsive to other cells, dividing and mutating out of sync with other cells; often they proliferate far quicker, which on many occasions causes cancers to turn into lumps under the skin. On most occasions, which are daily, rogue cells appear but are engulfed by WBCs and removed without any harm done.

Inflammation (inflammatory response)

The process of inflammation is to repair areas of the body that are under extra friction; this could be due to poor posture or excessive repetitive movements. Imagine the fan on a car's engine wasn't working – over time or on long drives the car is more likely to overheat. Water in the engine is there to cool off the excess heat but cannot cool the engine quick enough, so the engine not only loses water but also has no cooling mechanism. When our joints are misaligned they can cause friction points in places not suitable for friction; therefore they are more susceptible to damage. Inflammation is released to heal an area, but if the injury keeps recurring or never heals properly then healing times will be extended and less effective.

The inflammatory response is similar to the fire service in that it is sent to an area of our body to extinguish the heat from the friction, placed on, for example, a joint. At complex joints there are friction pads, called bursas, which secrete fluid to lubricate the area to avoid excessive friction when the joint either moves or is under strain. However, as mentioned, when a joint is misaligned and repetitively used, the bursa is either overused or friction happens not on the bursa, instead at a less-cushioned area, not meant for friction.

Over time, if this isn't corrected the bursa cannot keep secreting fluid quick enough, to cool the area to avoid friction and damage. When the fire service (inflammatory response) arrives they cordon off the area (restrict movement) and spray the injury with inflammation, to cool the area. When the body heals the fire service will drain the inflammation from the area. In chronic cases it's not so simple: the fire (heat dissipated) is never fully put out, so healing takes longer, due to not enough rest or the cause of the problem hasn't been addressed.

This means the inflammation cannot be drained from the area and pouches or cysts of inflammation will form in the joint, making the joint look puffy, usually stiffening a joint's movement, which is painful to touch or on certain movements. Those pains are there to protect you from damaging the joint further. Compensatory movement of other joints will protect the injured joint; however, if the problem is not resolved, over time compensatory movements will eventually cause friction at other joints.

Even if a period of inactivity follows and the joint is able to drain the area, the likelihood is that when you return to activity the problem will return if the cause is not addressed, meaning a continuation of increased friction and inflammation.

A preferred method of strategy at this stage is a cortisone injection. I'm not absolutely against cortisone injections – in some cases they can offer a long-term solution, but they also can be a short-term fix. When inflammation cannot be drained, the old inflammation will become hard and sticky in the joint space.

The cortisone injection freezes the area so that fresh inflammation can penetrate and clean up the old dried and sticky inflammation. In these circumstances they can be useful, but they are only ever a time-limited solution. If the cause is not addressed, they risk this injury cycle happening again.

It's logical to think that another injection will reduce the pain like the first time, so the patient seeks another cortisone injection. The issue is that cortisone injections not only remove sticky, dried inflammation – they also remove the precious joint structure that the old inflammation is stuck to. For this reason multiple cortisone injections are not long-term solutions. The body will continue to produce inflammation as a protective mechanism until the cause is addressed.

The cortisone injection risks also removing the precious structure of the joint, which will cause arthritis there. A small calcium build-up will appear to replace the damaged structure, attempting to reduce the friction that was never addressed; this is commonly known as a bony spur.

This is far more serious than a bursitis. Without sounding like a broken record, this is what happens when the cause is not addressed – unnecessary wear and tear changes the structure of the joint, leading to eventual arthritis, not because of advancement in age but a lack of understanding of excessive friction in joints and a lack of understanding of how the body heals.

Summary

Phew! I feel like we went through a lot there. Inside all of us there is the quantum field which is a paradox within three-dimensional physics. Atoms combine to become molecules and they combine to eventually become bacteria and cells. This is the community inside all of us, working cooperatively together to maintain homeostasis for us and them.

The blood is the carrier for the oxygen, and immune and inflammatory responses, which are the tip of an iceberg of coordinated physiological processes. They support our internal world and life forces by creating a constant balance for our cells and bacteria to live within, with relatively little disturbance to our everyday life. They will compensate, neutralize and repair as they see fit, with little conscious input.

I've made a scientific and philosophical case here that these tiny organisms living inside us are not only intelligent but they are a possible seat for conscious consciousness not in the brain, as according to conventional thinking. What are your thoughts?

Microbiology quiz

1) The density of the atom is where?
a) The electron field
b) The nucleus
c) Electrons
d) The molecule

2) Electrons travel by?
a) Linearly orbiting the nucleus
b) Quantum leap
c) Car
d) Being limited to the speed of light

3) Homeostasis is described as?
a) Controlled by medication
b) A random bodily function
c) Cells frozen in time
d) The body balancing itself

4) Bacteria are?
a) Living organisms that are essential to our survival
b) A threat to human existence
c) Something we could live without
d) All bad for our health

5) The cell is?
a) Only found in prison
b) A biological living organism
c) A mechanical machine
d) Uncooperative with other cells

6) The cell membrane is?
a) The brain of the cell
b) Is un-commutative with other membranes
c) Allows anything object into the cells
d) Something that acts randomly

7) David Tennison proposes consciousness is where?
a) The brain
b) Outside of the body
c) The cell
d) In coffee (ask me in the morning and I might choose this one)

8) Blood is made of four parts: which of the following is not a part?
a) Plasma
b) Red blood cells
c) Platelets
d) Cartilage

9) The main function of blood is?
a) How nutrient and oxygen reach our cells
b) To keep carbon dioxide in the body
c) To repair broken bones
d) To break down foods

10) Inflammation is?
a) An annoying pain to be eradicated by anti-inflammatory medication
b) A cool area which feels nice with heavy pressure
c) A healing site for the body usually due to heat caused by friction
d) A healing site for the body usually due to heat caused by friction
e) A useless function and one we could live without like appendixes and tonsils

11) White blood cells are?
a) The body's immune response
b) They let invaders take up home inside us
c) Uncoordinated and with random function
d) Something only working during fight or flight

Biology

The stress and relaxation response

Before we can talk about how the systems of the body function we need to understand the stress response. It's more commonly known as fight or flight, in response to a perceived danger, or rest and digest, which is the relaxation response. This is covered in much detail in *The Back Doctor Secrets* (my first book, pages 45–60) but it's worth recapping this bodily chain reaction, which uses multiple systems to protect our survival from a potential threat in the environment.

When we are afraid of a perceived threat, real or not, our body's chemical reaction is real. When fight or flight is triggered, the nervous system releases adrenaline into the bloodstream, which quickens our heart rate, concentrating blood flow to our limbs, and as a consequence reducing blood flow to the digestive and sexual organs. We are more capable of physically protecting ourselves from harm when blood flows to our muscles and our digestive and immune functions are sacrificed. All adults will know the feeling of fight or flight by recalling a moment when they were suddenly scared. Responding to stress is a natural process for the body to go through; this function keeps us safe and alerts us to dangers in the environment.

When the threat in the environment passes and we feel safe again, we will revert to rest and digest. Blood flow will be concentrated in our organs in the abdomen, instead of our limbs. We will feel like eating, be able to cry or use the toilet, whereas the opposite is true when we are experiencing fight or flight. The stress or relaxation (growth) response is one or the other, as we cannot be in both states at the same time. The stress response is a switch that needs to be turned off once the threat has passed so that the body can revert and recover; however, some people are so overwhelmed they are in a constant state of fear, meaning they cannot turn off the stress response.

When I typically experience the stress response I feel my heart quicken and I will take sharp inhales when I breathe. I feel tightness in my throat area above the heart, a disorientated feeling in my stomach, and my jaw will clench. The effects of adrenaline mean I lose my appetite, my concentration levels diminish, my attention becomes skittish and it's difficult to settle. After the adrenaline wears off I will feel shaky, cold and exhausted.

I usually reduce any causative stimuli to help me switch back to the relaxation response. I know when I'm returning to the relaxation response: I will yawn, feel my belly grumble, which might be accompanied by a sensation of needing to burp, and I will feel like eating. I can settle as my concentration returns and I can focus my attention.

Think of fight or flight (the stress response) in society such as during the Second World War. In the UK all resources went to the war effort (emergency measures), and events like the Olympics were postponed. The country amassed significant debt in protection of people's lives and liberty. When the war ended the country was able to return to rest and digest, the emergency was over and resources could be focused on growth and recovery. This took time because post war our resources were exhausted. In time we recovered and so did the world, and events like the Olympics resumed. This war lasted for almost six years but imagine if the war had never ended: that is what being stuck in fight or flight is like.

As I said, fight or flight is not good or bad; it is just a reaction to our environment and in some instances could save our lives. The problem arises when we are under constant stress – we do not switch back to rest and digest, for essential growth and maintenance. Over time, our physical health will decline, leaving us susceptible to illness which can be traced back to unresolved and constant psychological stresses triggering the fight or flight response.

Rest and digest	Fight or flight
Blood flows to organs normal	Blood flows to limbs ready to run, protect or attack
Blood pressure and pulse are normal	Blood pressure and pulse raises
Sexual function is normal	Sexual function reduces
Digestion is normal	Digestion reduces
Immune system is normal	Immune function is reduced

Systems

In the last chapter we learnt how the world of the small is made up of trillions of tiny cells, which are only possible to view under a microscope and are stacked on top of one another to make us. When those cells come together they form larger objects that can seen with the naked eye, such as our skin, bones and internal organs. Every part of us is part of a system to perform a function, which in turn helps another system. Each system performs its own specialization to combine with complex multi-layered integrative systems.

Systems are like letters of the alphabet that work in sync, coming together to produce words and sentences to take on more meanings than their individual letters can on their own. This combining of function from the small to the large is how life works. For example, A, B, C are just individual letters, but arrange them to spell CAB, and now the letters could describe a taxi.

There is no language without these individual parts. This is the same with all systems: their individual parts become more than their sum through multiple interactions. They work with other systems with a similar or opposite function, to create the many cogs of multiple, higher-level systems that work together for life to function seamlessly.

The skeletal and the muscular systems are an example of opposite strengths working together to provide bodily function. Bone is strong but cannot contract, whereas muscle is flexible and can contract, pulling like rope to shorten. These two opposite functions of bone and muscle are complimentary and are what facilitates movement and maintains our posture.

The two opposite performing systems working in tandem means we can run, walk and jump, but also manage activities like chewing our food or breathing, which are also controlled by muscular function attached to bone. If either of these systems is malfunctioning, such as with a muscular strain for instance, the movements we make would be impaired or not possible.

Our organs' individual function combines together, with other organs to function within larger systems. There are eleven systems in the body, this is the story of us and how we work. Each organ within a system is relying on another organ to function at their best possible level. I will attempt to explain a few of main organs and their relationship with others organs in their systems, to view them specifically and holistically.

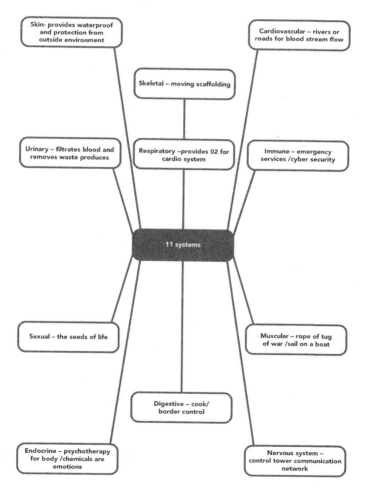

The priority systems and their related organs sustain life and homeostasis. These are the nervous, endocrine, respiratory, cardiovascular and digestive systems, which we will focus on here. All systems sustain life but these few are the most vital. To discuss all the organs individually and specifically is a book in itself. Instead, this chapter will provide the essentials, as well as an interesting overview of how the inside world interacts by means of communication, transportation and energy conversion.

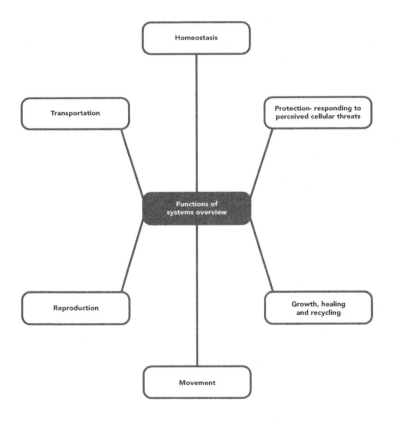

Electrics

You've got a nerve

The nervous system consists of the brain, the brain stem, spinal cord and spinal nerves. The brain consists of 100 billion neurons that we are issued with at birth. Most other cells in the body will last no more than a couple of weeks or months but neurons, although their components might change, are in essence the same cells we start our life with, and therefore they do not regenerate as well as other cells when damaged.

If neurons are deprived of oxygen they will die or be permanently damaged within minutes. People who sustain serious head injuries can be left with life-changing effects to their faculties for this reason. The spinal nerves are more capable of regenerating but significantly less in comparison to the healing time of a muscular tear, which can regenerate more quickly because muscles have a different type of cell with a rich blood supply.

Our brain

The brain itself weights approximately three pounds and is mostly water and spinal fluid. It's a porous structure, similar to the consistency of a saturated sponge; in this state the brain is not only one of the largest organs, but is also the most vital to living. The brain is the royalty of all organs; in survival situations, your innate intelligence will sacrifice blood flow to your limbs and other organs to prioritize blood flow to the brain. When people go into shock their skin will often turn blue in colour because blood flow is being diverted to the organs as a priority over the limbs.

If you read my first book then you'll know that I've competed in ju-jitsu, which is mixture of judo and wrestling, with a focus on chokes and limb locks. Someone being choked will usually tap their opponent in time before becoming unconscious, but if they are new to the sport they will fight on and eventually become temporally unconscious because oxygen is being cut from the brain due to the neck choke. If blood flow to the brain is interrupted for the briefest moment our body goes into survival mode and consciousness is the first luxury to go.

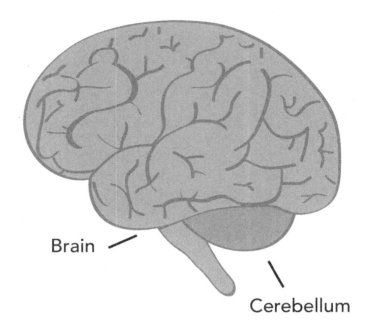

Brain

Cerebellum

It's complicated

The brain's anatomy can get quite funky and complicated. It's certainly the most researched organ but also the least understood. Most other organs can be complicated at times but their overall function is generally mechanical and linear, making them easier to understand. The brain however is mysterious and many brain functions are counterintuitive. We can observe it's the nerve centre, but we go no further, meaning that when we think and feel the brain lights up on an MRI scan, associating neurons with those thoughts and feelings. We can locate where memories are likely to be stored but no one has ever found an actual memory or consciousness in the brain.

Royal Highness

Our royal organ has a penthouse apartment, called the cranial vault (the inside of the skull), which is protected by a royal guard and a taster, called the blood brain barrier, which stops or controls the passage of certain materials into the brain. As one might expect of someone of high society, the brain is also a picky eater and will only accept glucose for sustenance; therefore glucose and oxygen are VIPs, passing freely with no need for an appointment, although many are refused entry. Antibiotics or therapeutic drugs for brain cancers are to name a few on the 'never appointment' list. When the barrier is compromised by trauma, this tight control is weakened, letting inflammation or toxins reach the brain.

The spinal cord

The spinal cord is a minor royal, protected by bones called the spine or vertebral column. Within the spinal cord there are a hundred million neurons; it extends from the brain downward, through a hole in the vertebral column. Thirty-six individually moveable bones stack on top of one another, protecting the royal messages being passed through the spinal cord, while also allowing branches of peripheral nerves to leave the spinal cord like floors of an elevator.

The nerves are different to muscles in the sense that they do not stretch, similar to a cable of an electrical appliance. If the nerve is at risk of being damaged or stretched, your body will let you know, first by restricting movement, then secondly with pain signals. Pain is caused to protect you from doing any more harm to yourself.

Your body will restrict movement initially, but if the nerve continues to be stretched, muscles will go into spasm. The weight of a small coin on a nerve is enough to cause a muscle spasm. When the spinal column is aligned, nerve branches leaving the spinal cord will be at their optimal length. When we lose the shape of our spine, nerves are at risk of being stretched, twisted or having pressure placed on them.

There are two sets of peripheral nerves, 1) sensation and 2) motor, travelling along separate closed loop pathways. With electrical appliances power travels one way from the socket to the appliance but imagine a cable went from the appliance to the socket. In the body, power flows both ways through sensory and motor nerves. These electricity signals are called nerve impulses, travelling at 300 kilometres an hour.

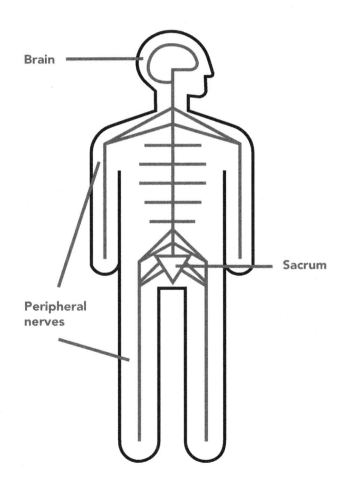

Sensory nerves are *yin*, passive, only receiving information – they can feel hot, cold, numbness, and pins and needles, to name a few sensations – whereas motors nerves are *yang*, actively instructing change, carrying the command to a muscle, organ or cell. An example is that when we become too hot, the sensory nerves alert the brain and motor nerves will turn on the sprinklers, by which I mean sweat glands.

When a signal is ready to be sent to the neurons, which are the cells of the nerves, they become polarized, connecting a negative and positive electrical charge, known as an action potential, which is like a Mexican wave, passing through each and every one of the neurons to reach the signal's destination. Imagine a set of dominoes in a row: when the first domino falls, a chain reaction begins, creating momentum for the others to fall.

The strength we can generate in our muscles is determined by harnessing these action potentials. The greater we can recruit action potentials will mean more muscle strength is available. When the signal reaches the nerve, the muscle will need to contract, lengthen or remain the same. The more control our nervous system has over our muscles, the greater the control and strength.

Synchronous activity within the nervous system not only recruits muscle but is also coordinates multiple muscles' contractions for complex movements such as walking or standing. This is one of numerous processes being managed by your innate intelligence, as well as monitoring our blood pressure, blood sugar levels, oxygen levels and carbon dioxide levels, to name a fraction of them.

A neuron works with other neurons, in unison, beyond conscious control, allowing autonomic functions to happen without much or any thought. Our nervous system is a computer program but not just any computer program; at present it's better than any artificial computer yet to be designed. Your biology is the greatest technology known today.

Reflexes

When you touch something hot and you instantly pull your hand away without realizing, this is called the withdrawal reflex. This protective mechanism will withdraw a limb faster than you feel pain; remember nerve signals are travelling at 300 kph; pain signals are slower and conscious consciousness is even slower.

It's similar to when a fuse box trips, as a failsafe to stop the wiring blowing in a house. The sensory nerves pick up on the danger and the limb is withdrawn by an immediate reflex. There are many reflexes in our body and if you've ever had them tested then you'll know this is one of the only acceptable times to hit someone with a hammer (a reflex hammer). The knee reflex's purpose is to help us remain standing, against the force of gravity. The acts of vomiting, coughing, sneezing, swallowing, urination and defecation all involve reflexes.

Plumbing

Pumps

There are two vital pumps that start the moment we leave the womb till the day we die. While we are alive these pumps will continuously work regardless of whether we are sleeping, eating or exercising. Even when you are sick they will be there for you, your whole life, never asking for time off, and they will both beating in rhythm continuously together. If these pumps fail for any reason the answer is not good and if they were to stop entirely for any reason, we would be dead in minutes. These pumps are the tireless blessings of the heart and lungs.

The lungs

Let's start with the lungs. There are two of them, situated within the chest, behind the ribcage and each lung is called a lobe. They are one kilo in weight, and when they inflate they will hold six litres of air. Within a lung is an airtight wall just like the pressure in a balloon, inflating and deflating with each breath. Air is sucked from the atmosphere, via muscle contractions. The diaphragm, positioned at the base of the lungs and ribcage, flattens to create suction on inhalation and expands on exhalation, forcing air out of the lungs.

When we exercise the demand for oxygen in the body increases, therefore our heartbeat quickens and so does our respiration. The diaphragm enlists help from other muscles in and around the ribcage, namely the neck muscles and intercostal muscles (muscles between the ribs). Our body needs to replace the increased oxygen consumption at cellular level and remove harmful carbon dioxide, especially if we want to maintain the work rate of exercise. A marathon runner can keep pace for the duration because they are restoring their oxygen levels as quick as they are using them. Their bodily respiration is keeping up with circulatory respiration, called aerobic fitness.

Hot air

Air travels through the nose, mouth and larynx, which is where our voice box is. Talking is like a wind instrument, as every time we pronounce a word or make a sound, this is caused by a muscle opening and closing in the larynx, supported also by the tongue and lips to make a desired sound via our vocal cords. Exhaled air is released from the body which is warmer than atmospheric air, so the sounds we make are really just hot air, and some of us are making more than others!

If your name's not down, you're not coming in

The respiratory system is picky about what is let into the lungs. That's why we grow nostril hair, sneeze or cough. They are the first line of the defence to stop any dust or harmful objects entering the space of the lungs. As we go inside past the nose and mouth, the tract that leads to the lungs is lined with tiny hair-like structures that catch anything that the first line missed. These tiny hairs can go into spasm causing restrictive breathing, commonly known as asthma.

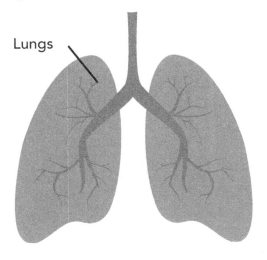

Lungs

In the diagram you can see that if were to turn the anatomy of the lungs upside down the trachea, which is the tube that connects our nose and mouth to our lungs, looks very similar to a tree trunk. The branches are the bronchi and the leaves are the alveoli, which is where the oxygen is taken from the air into the bloodstream, much in the same way that leaves catch sunlight.

The mighty heart

An adult heart is the size of a fist, situated within the ribcage and slightly left of centre. The left lung is smaller to accommodate the position of the heart. Weighing in at one pound but worth all the pounds in the world to you, I present the heart.

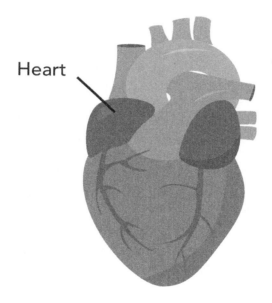

Heart

Hearts are unique because they form their own set of muscles, not found anywhere else in the body, called cardiac muscles. These are involuntary muscles and are governed by the chemicals in the blood and neurotransmitters (signals from the endocrine and nervous system). The cardiac muscles are a pacemaker for the heart to beat in rhythm. As mentioned earlier, hormones or nerve signals can either slow or speed up our heartbeat.

The heart is split into four quadrants of atriums and ventricles. Like many other parts of the body, the heart is split into pairs, as there is one atrium and one ventricle on each side of the heart. With only the volume of a grapefruit in the atrium and ventricle, these small but mighty quadrants, powered by muscles of the heart, beat on average 60-80 beats per minute at rest, to pump blood around the body and back to the lungs to be re-oxygenized.

The heart is the start and the end of the circulatory loop. Oxygen-rich blood is sent to our cells and exchanged for carbon dioxide, before travelling back to the heart for a small loop to the lungs to expel carbon dioxide and diffuse more oxygen, so that the blood becomes oxygen rich again. The blood travels along arteries that are supported by a contraction of muscles called peristalsis to increase blood flow, more commonly known as blood pressure. Arteries become smaller like a trunk of a tree becomes a branch and these branches are called capillaries.

Blood travels back to the heart via veins. Blood needs to travel from the lower limbs against the force of gravity, which is no mean feet, pun intended. This is managed by blood pressure in a closed loop system, therefore forcing blood back to the heart. Instead of veins contracting, their inside walls are lined with non-return valves, to stop blood flowing backwards, encouraging venous return. When we stand or walk the muscles in our legs contract, also increasing venous return, another good reason to move regularly.

If the heart was a business then it would most certainly trade in blood. At over 80% water, blood doesn't seem that special but our cells can't get enough and our heart keeps pumping to keep up with demand. Our Companies House trading stats are impressive, pumping 6-7 thousand litres of blood a day and with an annual turnover of 2.19-2.74 million litres a year.

Home is where the heart is

Imagine we lived in the heart and we went to visit our friend near the big toe. In the real world that journey might be a long drive into the countryside. We might drive on the motorway then through a town, a village, until we reach a single country lane where our friend lives. The motorways in this analogy are the arteries, the roads of the town are smaller, the village smaller yet and then the country lane is a capillary and the friend's house is a cell where the oxygen is dropped off and the carbon dioxide is collected, just like in the way that people leave their bins out to be collected. Our red blood cells are visitors, delivery drivers and bin disposal experts.

On the way home from our friends instead of going the way we came we take another route. Again we travel on the country lane, through the village, then a town, before getting onto the motorway and then home. On the way back blood travels along the veins. Capillaries, instead of becoming arteries, become veins and they get thicker the closer they get to the heart. As mentioned, veins differ from arteries in that there is no muscular contraction in the vein; instead there are non-return valves to aid venous return.

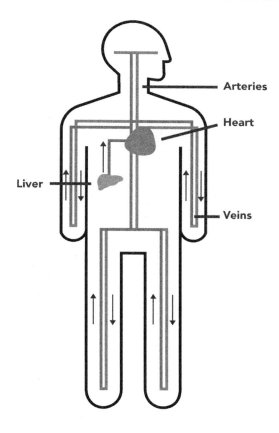

Alternative routes home

Blood fluid is also returned to the heart through the kidneys and lymphatic system. The kidneys come as a pair just like the lungs and are shaped like actual kidney beans. They are situated underneath the digestive organs, to the back of the body, just under the ribcage. The kidney's job is to filter our blood; to honour this high priority function our kidneys receive a whopping 20% of the total blood flow from the heart, similar to that of the brain.

The kidneys are like the lungs in reverse; instead of inhaling oxygen or expelling harmful carbon dioxide, a kidney will retain or remove chemicals from the blood depending on what is needed in the body. The lungs filter atmospheric air, whereas the kidneys filter blood of nutrients and waste. Too much sodium (the fancy name for salt) for instance will be removed; however, if there are low sodium levels, the kidneys will retain sodium in the bloodstream. Too much water or too little, the same order will apply.

Kidneys

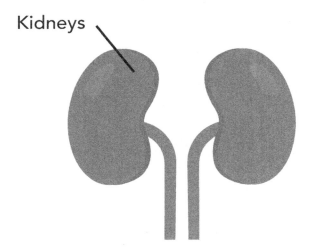

Excess water is formed into urine, containing chemicals surplus to requirements such as toxins to be removed from our body. The kidney is therefore the bathroom for the blood. All blood needs its toilet and wash breaks at some point throughout the day so that it feels refreshed for another loop.

Arterial flow – outbound

1. Oxygen-rich blood is taken to the left side of the heart for pumping around the body, which is vital for our cells to survive
2. Blood fills the atrium in preparation for the ventricles
3. The blood passes into the ventricles and when they contract the blood is forced into the aorta
4. The aorta ascends, splitting into smaller arteries to supply the brain, and descends to supply the rest of the body
5. Arteries become smaller and smaller until they are very tiny, becoming capillaries.

Venous return – inbound

1. Red blood cells not only attract oxygen but they also attract carbon dioxide so when oxygen is delivered to the cell, the red blood cell will load up on carbon dioxide
2. Blood is returned to the heart via the veins which work against gravity when standing
3. A combination of blood pressure in the closed loop, non-return valves in the veins and muscle contractions particularly in the legs help the blood back to the heart
4. The blood reaches the left side of the heart and is pumped back to the lungs
5. At the lungs red blood cells let go of the carbon dioxide and reload with oxygen
6. This completes our loop by returning back to the right side of the heart to do it all again
7. This cycle happens in a matter of minutes.

The internal internet

Within the nervous system, the brain acts as a control tower, sending and receiving messages, supported by the endocrine system. The nervous system can only send and receive electrical signals, whereas the endocrine system can send and receive electrical and chemical signals. The endocrine glands are dotted around the body, acting as our brain's corporals to maintain homeostatic ranges. The chemicals released by the endocrine system are manifested as feelings – the endocrine system is our mood maker.

The nervous and endocrine systems respond to stimuli by sending electrical impulses, which trigger the release of hormones or other chemicals into the bloodstream. The cardiovascular system provides the cells with their groceries. As mentioned earlier, the stress response sends an electrical and chemical signal to release adrenaline into the bloodstream. The nervous and endocrine systems need the cardiovascular system to enact their change. The network of the vascular system provides the roads and rivers to the body.

The nervous and endocrine systems act as a fast feedback system of instantaneous messages based on the information being received, whereas the cardiovascular one isn't a feedback system as such but it can reach the whole body through its network of ubiquitous vessels. The nervous and endocrine systems are the communication networks; the cardiovascular system provides the paths of transport for the nervous and endocrine systems to live vicariously through.

If the nervous system is the internet, the businesses on the internet are the endocrine system. When a user purchases a product from a business (endocrine system) an order is transferred from the internet website to the business's internal processing. The order will be packaged then shipped to wherever the postage address is listed. The endocrine system organizes this package (hormone release) and depending on the orders it receives from the internet (nervous system).

When a product is shipped from the endocrine glands, it will be transported by via the bloodstream. The cardiovascular system is all modes of transport. The hormones ordered will be stuck to red blood cells (container ships), along with oxygen and other nutrients; they are then shipped through to their location of delivery. All systems contribute to our overall health, but these systems in my opinion are the most vital to us, so my main focus has been to simplify them. They are so dependent on each other that they cannot function without the others long term.

Other worthy mentions – the digestive tract

The average bite to eat will take approximately 48 hours to go from your mouth to your anus. Chewing takes minutes but the rest of the digestive process savours a meal over many hours. The stomach for instance will dine on a meal for 3-6 hours, the small intestine 6-8 hours and the final stage in the large colon can be days, and this is where food becomes waste product.

There is a similar number of neurons in the digestive tract as there is in the spinal cord, known as the enteric nervous system. We do not even give a moment's conscious thought to that lovely meal we just ate because in the walls of the intestines is a network of neurons that will control the extraction of nutrients from our meals, so that our cells can dine too. Whether it's making sure we won't choke when swallowing, adding more acid or crushing in the stomach, or measuring the pressure of the intestines, the enteric nervous system has got this covered.

Food and mood

The enteric nervous system is closely linked to how we feel. When we do activities that are good for us, satisfying endorphins are released as a reward to remind us to do them again. When we eat food that is nutritious or when we eat with others (we are social animals) we feel good afterwards because of feel-good chemicals being released. A well-known chemical to be released is serotonin. When we eat carbohydrates, during or afterwards, serotonin is released, which causes a whoosh of satisfaction and relaxation. Similar to serotonin, other endorphins can act as natural painkillers.

Mastication

The mouth is the loading bay for the digestive tract, consisting of our lips, teeth, gums, tongue, uvula, saliva and bacteria. Chewing our food is called mastication. Muscles in our jaw compress our jagged teeth to tear and break food apart, in preparation for the stomach. In the mouth there are sensation receptors to subconsciously let us know when food is ready to be swallowed. These receptors can tell through a mouth full of food the current texture of its contents. Nuts for instance can be a risk for choking, so you will be compelled to chew for longer if those pieces of nuts are deemed too large by a receptor.

Taste buds

The tongue and the roof of the mouth is where our taste buds are. When we taste nice food the receptors in our mouth are the source of our enjoyment or not as may be the case. We can taste sweet, sour, salt, bitter and detect the texture of meat. Taste and smell work in tandem to recognize food sources that are safe to eat. Sour milk is an example of smell and taste working together because this alerts us that we might want to avoid ingesting this substance.

Taste buds will begin the sorting process using saliva, enzymes and bacteria to prep food for the stomach. For example, when we eat carbohydrate, an enzyme (a chemical to speed up other chemical reactions) is released in the mouth to begin the process of digestion that is not released when we eat protein.

Down the hatch

When a meal descends from our mouth, food enters the second part of the digestive tract, called the oesophagus, which is a long tube connecting our mouths to our stomachs. In the wall of the oesophagus are smooth muscles, which contract in a rhythmical action called peristalsis. These smooth muscles also form tight endings between organs, called sphincters, which control the flow of digestion, which I go into more detail in a few paragraphs below.

Food is prevented from entering the lungs by a trap door called the epiglottis. Air sneaks underneath the epiglottis into the lungs, whereas food falls on top and then descends into the oesophagus.

Stomach contents

By the time food reaches the stomach, mastication in the mouth has crushed and ripped it into smaller pieces, which have then been squeezed by peristalsis in the oesophagus. If that isn't enough, the stomach will now not only beat and crush food with repeated strong muscular contractions, but food will dramatically be dropped into hydrochloric acid.

The stomach is situated below the heart and lungs at the base of the sternum and is 1.4 litres in volume. The walls of the stomach are lined with a slime to protect them from the acid contents of the stomach. Stomach ulcers form when the slime is not being produced to protect the stomach wall and as a consequence acid burns through the lining. I'm sure we can all agree the last thing you want is acid being where it's not supposed to be.

Other than breaking food down further, stomach acid will kill any harmful bugs to save them reaching the small intestine and preventing stomach bugs or food poisoning. After a meal the stomach will expand and feel-good chemicals are released to signal we are full and satisfied.

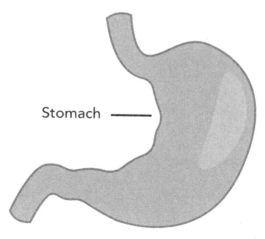

Stomach ———

Sphincters

At each end of the stomach is a sphincter, which is like a tiny fastener that stops the contents passing through quicker than the digestive process needs. Sphincters are found throughout the gastrointestinal and urinary tract. They are involuntary, which means they are controlled by the autonomic nervous system (subconscious control) but our emotions can affect them too. For instance, when we feel stressed we go to the toilet more often or less often. They are linked to the stress and relaxation response mentioned at the start of the chapter.

Many hands make light work

The small intestine is a long thin tube of approximately 23 feet in total. This is where the work of mastication, peristalsis and stomach pumping begins to pay off. Within the walls of the long squishy tubes are tiny cilia. Imagine tiny hands on the inside surface of the tube sorting through the nutrients, similar to how a picker would pick strawberries or any kind of fruit when in season. The picked nutrient is sent to the liver via the bloodstream for further processing, to be used as instant energy or stored.

Enzymes are released to dissolve the food further into smaller particles for energy release. When enough nutrients are extracted, peristalsis (muscle contraction) will move food along, making the belly grumble as they say. Not all extraction of nutrient takes place here, as some foods, such as fibre, will need to be broken down in the large intestine.

Irritable bowel syndrome and the like are usually caused by tiny tears on the surface of the tubing that is normally protected by a gooey surface, just like in the stomach. A common cause of these stomach and digestive issues is by being stuck in the stress response. This lack of internal maintenance can be due to lifestyle or mindset (stress response management).

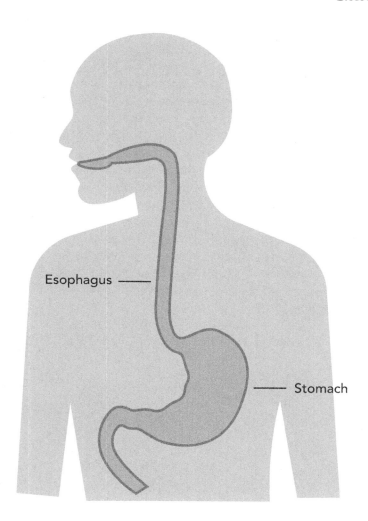

Esophagus ———

——— Stomach

The liver

The liver is the brain of the digestive system. It's so important that if our liver was to shut down we would be dead in minutes. It's really a dark horse because ask most people what the liver does and most will know it's important but will struggle to know why.

Positioned under the ribs on the right side of the body, the liver is the heaviest of all the organs, mainly because a quarter of your blood is flowing through the liver at any one time. It is the only internal organ which can regenerate. Nutrient-filled blood from the intestines flows through veins to the liver in preparation for venous return to the heart. The liver chooses what will go into the bloodstream and what nutrients will be stored there, depending on the demands of the body. The liver is a Michelin star chef, checking every meal before it is served.

Vitamins are stored in the liver and toxins can be filtered out of the bloodstream. The liver aids digestion by producing digestive juices, hormones and bile proteins. Stored fat and carbohydrates are converted into glucose, which if you remember is the preferred source of fuel for the brain, but also the heart and red blood cells. The liver will monitor the glucose levels to maintain homeostasis. Someone can develop a fatty liver when the fat stores of a liver are not being used, usually to protect the rest of the body from increased lipids in the bloodstream.

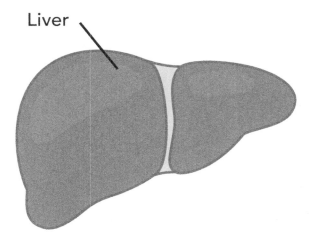

Liver

Large intestine

The bowel or large intestine and colon as it's also known is shorter than the small intestine, approximately six feet in total, but is wider in girth, with a thicker outer wall. The nutrients not absorbed through the small intestine are salvaged here by bacteria to maximize the energy consumed from food. The bacteria create a gas chamber to extract the final nutrients, which can take weeks, but most food sources pass through more quickly.

Once all nutrients have been extracted from food, what's left becomes waste product and leaves the body via the toilet. Our bowel movements are a good indicator of how healthy we are. When we are sick our stools will be watery, called diarrhoea, because the large intestine is not digesting food normally; or the opposite is when the stool is too hard, which will cause constipation.

Summary

As mentioned at the start of this chapter, this isn't a comprehensive list of the organs and systems; instead it is a breakdown of the most essential functions. Throughout the chapter I've given real world examples of when systems go wrong, usually because we are stuck in the stress response, so our body is unable do the house cleaning, such as producing protective slime onto the stomach and intestinal walls. These functions are less of a priority than our survival and that is the reason I opened the chapter with a brief understanding of the stress and relaxation response, before explaining the mechanics of the systems we have covered.

Being stuck in the stress response is like driving a car in first gear on the motorway and attempting to keep up with the other cars in higher gears. Eventually the high revs will make the car's engine overheat at the very least and will cause undue wear and tear. Switching gears in a combustion engine can utilize the momentum of the wheels, saving energy and reducing friction on the cogs of the engine. My advice is to learn the gears of the relaxation and stress response so our systems can run our engine efficiently for the long term.

Biology quiz

1) Fight or flight is?
a) A superhero's powers
b) Evolutionary bodily response to perceived threat to life
c) In-flight entertainment
d) The state we want to stay in most of the time

2) Rest and digest is?
a) Feeling stressed
b) Feeling scared
c) The body house cleaning
d) Something that weakens the immune system

3) When we are healthy a bodily system is?
a) A coordinated set of functions towards a purpose
b) An uncoordinated set of function without a purpose
c) Something that works independently of itself and take advantage of other systems
d) Something that works better with regular medication

4) The master system of the body is known as?
a) Urinary
b) Skeletal
c) Muscular
d) Nervous

5) When we are healthy our organs?
a) Work on a shift pattern
b) Never take a rest
c) Work when they want
d) Work once their invoice has been paid

6) Which organ is not part of the cardiovascular system?
a) Heart
b) Kidney
c) Lungs
d) Capillaries

7) Which organ pumps blood around the body?
a) Lungs
b) Liver
c) Heart
d) Kidney

8) Both lungs can contain how many litres of air?
a) 0.5
b) 1
c) 6
d) 10

9) Which vessels carry blood away from the heart?
a) Arteries
b) Capillaries
c) Veins
d) Arterioles

10) Which vessels carry blood back to the heart?
a) Capillaries
b) Veins
c) Arteries
d) Muscles

Systems continued
The healthcare system and introduction to the Hybrid Practitioner

Healthcare past, present and future

In the last three chapters I've explained the philosophy of individual and collective health and the immeasurable effect of a supporting or hindering mindset. Understanding and encouraging life forces with a positive mindset are cornerstones in maintaining and increasing the likelihood of a long and healthy life.

I dedicated chapters to explain how the body is innately intelligent, with many working parts smaller than the eye can see in which living organisms in themselves are working towards a shared economy. I've described how the body is similar to an engine with multiple parts working together to combine into multi-layered systems. I will now hold the healthcare system up against these working parts within us and compare and contrast to show the disparity, as healthcare does very little to support these life forces until symptoms arise.

The current healthcare model views the body as a machine (not utilizing the wisdom of the last two chapters), waiting until a person is sick before acting. This conditions people to not think proactively about their health because the healthcare system says they are healthy. How many times do we hear people say 'my doctor said I'm fine', even though they are still suffering with pain and symptoms? In the medical model, musculoskeletal pain is seen as an inevitability as we age and my aim is to show you this isn't always the case.

I will then present my own suggested changes for a proactive healthcare system, which is a cause and patient-centred approach, to work in accordance with our life forces and a strategy to maintain our health throughout a lifetime and not only when we are sick.

The past

The history of healthcare is curiously littered with treatments that are looked back on as odd by today's standards. However, in their day these treatments held strong support and validity, making them ubiquitous throughout the medical profession. Healthcare has reluctantly moved with the times and current understanding.

In the past there was limited knowledge of microbiology, biology and pharmacology. There were no antibiotics, paracetemol or anti-inflammatory drugs. There was little understanding of the function of cells and anything smaller than the eye could see. Seeing a doctor in the not-too-distant past could well mean bloodletting was considered the best course of action...

Bloodletting (until 1920)

Bloodletting was a favourite of medical practitioners for a few hundred years. It was the go-to for everything, much in the same way antibiotics are today. Bloodletting is exactly that, taking a lancet and drawing blood from a vein. In earlier chapters I explained the vital functions of blood and how they are the container ships so oxygen and nutrients can reach our cells; therefore removing blood from an already sick person does more harm than good.

As a result this procedure was never proven but was a mainstay for a long time. In an age when there was no consciousness of the need to keep things sterile, opening a vein ran the risk of secondary infections and God knows how many unnecessary deaths were due to this procedure.

Here's a quote from Hornblower, the commodore in a series of novels by C. D. Forester based during the Napoleonic Wars. Captain Hornblower has been wounded in battle:

His sleeve was rolled up above the elbow, and the surgeon, lancet in hand, was about to open a vein to bleed him. Hornblower withdrew his arm abruptly, for he did want to be touched by that thing, nor by those hands which were black with other men's blood. (from *Admiral Hornblower*)

Mental/lunatic asylums

In the Victorian era there were as many mental health institutions (asylums) as there are hospitals today. They were grand buildings for people with diagnoses such as depression and feeble-mindedness. There was no other adequate treatment for people with mental health issues, other than to send them away. Even when I was growing up in the 1990s the medical profession still refuted that our thoughts and feelings affect our physical health and there is still resistance today.

Although there is more awareness of mental health now, treatment usually means medication instead of asylums, which still does not address the cause of the person's mental health. Diagnoses are right, but the treatments they prescribe are to control symptoms instead of resolving them.

Lobotomies (1936–1967)

The lobotomy is one of the biggest healthcare mistakes of the 20th century – answer on a postcard if you can think of one bigger. At least bloodletting in most cases didn't guarantee leaving a person with no faculties and brain damaged. This procedure involved taking a person with a mental health disorder and hammering a metal spike through the eye socket to puncture the frontal lobe, curing them of their mental health issue, but also curing them of all their cognitive function.

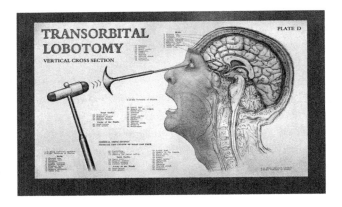

Surprisingly (sarcasm alert), effectively driving an axe into someone's brain made the recipient become a vegetable for the rest of their life. An absolute failure and it is now defunct but this procedure was valid and maintained as being beneficial for many years, even though it was wrecking people's health.

Had lobotomies been allowed to continue, they were seen as a eugenic technique for sedation of the elderly so their end-of-life care was less expensive, to solve hyperactivity in children and to control gambling and drug addiction. A shock therapy sending an electrical current into the brain is still used today.

Eugenic thinking

After Darwin's theory of evolution had been accepted, a popular belief emerged in medicine and science that if we are evolving then they could play God by controlling who could breed, therefore creating a better society. Eugenicists produced a body of scientific 'evidence' that a person deemed to have inferior genes was harming society. They proposed a program of **forced sterilization** that would reduce crime and disability, and the traits of weaker mental character would be eradicated.

Eugenics and **forced sterilization** were proved to be a flawed concept as well as being inhumane but not before thousands were sterilized against their will and unjustly. Deciding if someone needed to be sterilized or not was open to discrimination; people could be sterilized based solely on their accent or the colour of their skin. Eugenics was stretched even further in Nazi Germany when the theory was applied to minority races such as Jews and traveller people to protect the Aryan race by mass genocide.

Amazingly healthcare is still using eugenic thinking by making assumptions regarding our genes: that if there is a family history of such and such, in later life you are likely to experience the same illness. As I explained in biology (epigenetics page XXX) there are no genes that turn on at birth for heart disease or cancer, they only turn on throughout a lifetime which is usually due to stress and the belief that they will happen because healthcare tells us this is to be true.

100 years from now

How many medical prescriptions, procedures and surgeries we see today will be redundant in 100 years, viewed as useless in the same way we view the above mentioned, along with leaching and prescribing mercury? With hindsight these practices seem strange; we question how could we persist for so long with these oddities.

A few examples of today's persistence in such oddity are the overuse of pain medication, antibiotics and unnecessary surgeries – and the suppression of lifestyle modifications in favour of preventative medication that is inferior in comparison to exercise.

What is true today is replaced with a better practice or procedure tomorrow. It is just a question of when. I hate to break the news but the modern healthcare system is on more than a few occasions getting it wrong. Let's look at today's potential prize contenders:

Today's questionable practices

Antibiotics (overuse)

When penicillin was mass produced in the 1940s it was a genuine wonder drug because it could target and destroy bacteria, previously untreatable. Certain infections would likely kill people before antibiotics, and then suddenly they routinely survived. It was and still is a fantastic achievement by the scientists involved and they were justly awarded a Nobel Prize in 1945.

Alexander Fleming, probably the most famous of the three scientists to receive Nobel prizes for this achievement, said in his acceptance speech that bacteria could become immune to antibiotics with overuse, adding predicting the future to Fleming's many talents. Antibiotics are now being overused and bacteria are becoming resistant to them. The numbers of people suffering and dying with infections that used to routinely survive is increasing, the situation regressing due to antibiotics being unable to stop previously treatable bacteria.

The overuse is partly from the medical profession, overprescribing in many cases to people with issues that antibiotics will not solve, like a viral infection. However the biggest culprit is the agricultural industry. Brace yourself here: a whopping 70% of all the world's antibiotics are given to livestock, not because they are suffering a bacterial infection but to promote growth and as a precaution against them acquiring an infection. We in the process are eating secondary antibiotics for this reason. And it doesn't take a genius to work out why antibiotics are less effective than they used to be.

Opioids (overuse)

Next is the overuse of opioids, which are highly addictive medications derived from the plant that also makes heroin. They were primarily only designed for short-term use; however, they are being used for a wide range of long-term chronic pain cases. People are prescribed opioid medication to mask their pain and are not addressing the underlying cause.

Long-term use means they need to increase their opioid dose because the pain eventually returns. Now they are taking more pain medication to mask the symptoms and are more likely to become hopelessly addicted to them. This resulted in an estimated 250,000 deaths from opioid overdoses between 1999 and 2014.

This is another example of the pitfalls of dealing with the symptoms and not the cause. The opioids are a short-term fix, temporarily resolving the symptoms, but in time the original problem returns, to be accompanied by a secondary problem (an addiction) that is a direct result of the misuse of this medication.

A lack of tonsils, appendix and too much surgery?

A study conducted at the Karolinska Institute in Stockholm in 2011 discovered people with their tonsils removed at a young age are 44% more likely to suffer a heart attack in later life than people still with their tonsils intact. The same research found people who still had their appendix as they aged were 33% less likely to suffer a heart attack. These organs of the body provide immune functions that are lost when they are removed.

Having been a practitioner for some time now, I can't but feel that many surgeries could be prevented by a proactive model of healthcare and a conservative approach to slow the progression of arthritic joints. I've seen patients' X-rays of the hip joints pre op and yes there is damage to the joint but on closer inspection the other side is in exactly the same condition but without pain. A new hip joint only lasts ten years on average. Wouldn't doing everything possible to resolve the hip pain before going under the knife for an irreversible, life-changing operation, especially in those of younger in age, be preferable?

Through developing my own techniques, I've seen the power of aligning and restoring function to the spine and hips. I feel that in the future if people like myself and our techniques can be utilized and recognized as an intervention before surgery, then I am in no doubt we could prevent surgeries that are seen as absolute necessary today.

Flu vaccines?

It may surprise you that there has never been a long-term clinical trial to study if flu vaccines are effective or not. Their only proof is they may lessen a person's symptoms; they are unproven to stop transmission or contraction. Even if vaccines do lessen the symptoms there is a risk reward, in the sense that to avoid flu of short duration, a person risks lifelong side effects and disability from the vaccine.

Think of the Hippocratic code of 'first do no harm' and the Nuremburg code, created after the Second World War, so that people were never again forced or coerced into medical treatments or experiments against their will. When people are being coerced and in some cases worse, being injured by the vaccine, I question are immunization programs breaking these codes? What would Winston Churchill make of these encroachments on civil liberties?

Questioning the effectiveness of vaccines is a taboo subject. People are being convinced they work, are encouraged not ask not to questions of their effectiveness or their safety, and instead we must take the testimony of the vested interests of manufacturers, without independent reviews. Governments and mainstream media are touting them as the only scientific solution to preventative care. It is not science if we cannot question their scientific robustness. This lack of ability to discuss flu vaccines in scientific terms is what makes me question the situation.

If they are valid scientifically why is any negative data that questions their effectiveness suppressed and replaced by misinformation? Why is blatant coercion being used to encourage a traditionally liberal and free society (the UK) into immunization programs? If vaccines are safe and effective what is there to hide?

zIn some cases people are more likely to be injured and suffer a lifelong disability due to a vaccine than suffering unduly from the infection the vaccine is meant to protect them from. This means some vaccines present more risks than the particular infection they are designed to protect against.

I support anyone's choice to be vaccinated, but don't stop there. A vaccine will protect us against one infection, whereas lifestyle modifications (exercise and diet) and a positive mindset will protect us against all infections but also prevent disease and increase our lifespan. I suggest taking the exercise vaccine daily.

The status quo

My background is in personal training and chiropractic. In both fields I've always thought outside the box beyond the limitation to what was already known in those professions. I found that once I understood them, they complimented each other, whereas my lecturers hadn't even considered this combination. If people exercised regularly within their limits, they were more likely to hold their adjustments. Based on this premise I focused my energy on a sequence of adjustments that would return someone to fitness in the fastest way possible. The result was the The Back Doctor Technique, which I use in my clinic.

From designing my own technique, with time and reflection, I was able to improve incrementally towards a holistic model; however, I know there is more room for improvement within my system. Those improvements can only happen when the healthcare system makes the inevitable shift from a disease-centric model, towards a holistic, proactive one. Once testing equipment and procedures can be accessed or they have integrated holistic practitioners through the NHS budget, only then can we move to the next stage of healthcare, where new and better ways of treating patients that do not exist at present will become available.

Imagine taking a car to be serviced by a mechanic and they refused to service the car because there was nothing wrong presently when driving. The current healthcare model will not service us unless we present with symptoms; in the absence of symptoms we are considered healthy. Without a label or diagnosis to express a problem of our functions and feedback, the healthcare system takes no action.

When we are given labels and diagnoses we are usually already sick and a pharmaceutical treatment plan is administered to fit your label or diagnosis. The meaning of health in our current model is 'if it isn't broke, don't fix it' and when it does break pharmaceuticals are then the main options. This is a reactionary and counterproductive model of healthcare without prevention in mind, other than through immunization programs.

In the absence of symptoms we are considered healthy, but disease manifests over time and not at the moment when we are given a diagnosis. The current model discounts thoughts, feelings and emotions from consideration and only focuses on isolated biological changes as markers of health. This mechanistic view treats the body like a machine instead of a living organism, therefore missing the period of dis-ease (loss of psychological wellbeing) where a holistic approach is likely to solve the issue.

To wait until our health breaks down is not in our best interests as some symptoms and diseases are irreversible and progressive. The current healthcare model is working in the interests of pharmaceutical companies that are driven to tender contracts (paid through our taxes) from the government and make large profits for their shareholders. Their dominance has many influential patrons within SAGE and the NHS, who advise the government to spout limiting beliefs to stifle a proactive model of healthcare.

As mentioned in the philosophy chapter, this encourages an outside-in perspective, that people just need a pill or a vaccine to solve all their problems. This encourages people in the stage before disease when they are not well to not read the signs and act upon them; instead they wait until symptoms persist or worsen and then expect to be prescribed medication when they see a medical professional.

How many times do we hear people say 'I just need a course of antibiotics and I'll be OK'? These people are the unfortunate victims of a warped system to make them dependant on a healthcare system not working in their interests, which isn't 'free' as many people believe – this is funded through our taxes. Our expectation of a 'free' service is a barrier to improving healthcare.

Patients are encouraged to wait for symptoms but they could have been unhappy for some time in a job or relationship so when they become sick, instead of tracing the cause back to their origins, they are instead told they are an innocent victim of 'some bad genes', absolving them of responsibility. This makes the patient feel better initially, that they are not the cause or responsible for their illness, but this misdirects away from the psychological component that may well have caused the illness in the first place.

The patient is then branded with a permanent eugenic label which follows them for the rest of their life. Their autonomy to recognize their own situation and take responsibility for their health is taken away by this label that they are victim to their genes. The irony is the label cocoons them in certainty which makes them feel better but is potentially doing more harm than good long term.

This is the conditioning of those limiting beliefs filtering down through to the patient. The medical professional over many years tells a patient 1) wait until you're sick 2) long-term industrial medication is the cure and 3) you are a victim to your genetics and will become sick in a certain timescale (see the nocebo effect section in the philosophy chapter). Over time these limiting beliefs become second nature to lay patients. People do not act proactively towards their health because they are told not to do so, and in doing so they become passive hypochondriacs, unable to help themselves because they are being told to believe this is normal.

Modern medicine has had a positive effect on our lives but I disagree with the belief that healthcare is perfect and cannot be constructively criticized. Instead we are told to worship healthcare as some kind of unquestionable deity. Let me bust some of modern medicine's myths:

Myth 1: Modern medicine is a miracle of why we live longer

Modern medicine for crisis and emergency care is a miracle; many lives are saved that would have been lost in previous years, but this is only one factor in why we live longer. Our standard of living has improved greatly in the last 100 years. Most homes are centrally heated, and electricity and refrigeration are affordable amenities to most people in the UK. We also are able to separate drinking and waste water through flushing toilets, plumbing and a sewage system.

Myth 2: Holistic health is hippy nonsense

Thinking holistically about the body is backed by science. Lifestyle modifications (holistic changes) are valid scientifically, but unfortunately they cannot be patented and turn a profit, so this science is stigmatized by those that stand to gain from other 'science' being the gold standard. If you express a holistic mindset then you are painted as someone that must be away with the fairies, which is a weak straw man argument that has traction in public opinion. This is parroted without any validity by the healthcare patrons where they can misdirect their audience because of their limited knowledge.

Myth 3: Natural remedies are nonsense

The ancient worlds of antiquity used natural remedies as medication; the Egyptians alone had 700 known natural remedies for healing, the Romans recorded their uses in books and the Greeks had the first hospitals. Most pharmaceutical medication is derived from plants; why therefore is there a belief that natural remedies are useless? Natural remedies could be useful if administered earlier in people's dis-ease but when they are really sick the window for them becomes smaller.

Skilful marketing and pharmaceutical rhetoric is creating the perception that natural remedies are of no value. All vitamins and minerals can be obtained from a balanced diet, whereas there is no nutritional value in pharmaceutical medication. We are living through a period of medical mystification to not trust ourselves and instead trust what we are being told.

Myth 4: A proactive healthcare system would be cost prohibitive

Having people healthy throughout their lifetime would cost less than waiting until people are sick and then putting them on a lifetime of medication. An initial investment would be needed to set a new system up focusing on education, proactive wellness and understanding patient psychology. In time the annual budget would reduce because people would be less likely to become sick in their prime to later years. Healthcare education beginning from childhood would eventually filter through, making a happier and a more responsible society.

These dogmas are slowing the progression towards a holistic, proactive healthcare system. If you hear someone parroting the nonsense of these myths, please hand them this book.

The healthcare budget

Practitioners like myself are currently outcasts from NHS resources or budgets (£133 billion), unless you are a medical doctor working within the NHS. It's unlikely that as a chiropractor or an osteopath you will be able to access these resources, certainly not without incurring a charge for the patient, or needing to subscribe to the current healthcare model (outside-in approach).

I myself would not give up my principles or values to work within the reactive model of care dominated by the pharmaceutical industry. Chiropractic philosophy is about an inside-out approach to health, which I subscribe to. This means I believe health comes from within and not from a pill only when we are sick, which is an outside-in approach. The former is productive and proactive and the latter is counterproductive and reactive by waiting for symptoms to arise.

Modern medicine has created a system where between healthcare services and the pharmaceutical companies they are absolutely in control of the healthcare train set. Patronage decides who can be involved, influencing policy decision makers with monetary rewards, encouraging the removal of anyone prepared to speak out against them, replacing them with patrons who will agree to their terms, controlling education for student doctors and encouraging patient expectation to be 'pills are what you need'.

Complimentary alternative therapies like chiropractic are usually small businesses, family run, and they are cut off at the knees from the testing and resources that are at the fingertips of those in the pharmaceutical medical profession.

I did a dissertation on an initiative called 'any qualified provider', which was a patient-centred approach, designed to allow patients to choose the best course of care for them. A patient would go to their GP, requesting to see a chiropractor, osteopath or acupuncturist, and so on. I was excited about this because at face value this was a move towards a holistic healthcare model.

What my dissertation found was that 'any qualified providers' was a facade. Applicants had to be cleared by a panel of medical practitioners and physiotherapists, and surprise surprise, they would only accept physiotherapists onto the list, and justified this by saying GPs were only comfortable working with physiotherapists as they didn't understand the other professions. This is what we are up against; even when the policy advocates for inclusion, they will close ranks.

In my proposed future, the healthcare system would be

removed from the capitalist market, funded in the same way the NHS is funded today, but the budget would also control research. Where will this money come from, you ask? Well, most holistic sciences and research costs a fraction of the price of expensive drug trials and the research for proactive interventions (lifestyle modifications) already exists, but this is being suppressed by the current reactionary model by those who stand to gain from this status quo, namely the pharmaceutical industry and their patrons within medicine.

From my dissertation it was clear, Big Pharma as it is known has complete dominance over healthcare and government policy, acting like a cartel with its NHS patrons. Over the last 60 years they have handed out large bonuses to doctors who encourage their drugs, paying doctors to author papers that they did not write, and they are prepared to pay the fines for unlawful practices, known in the industry as the cost of doing business.

In a holistic NHS, the focus will be on prevention rather than a cure or management programs for symptoms only when we are sick. In the beginning investment would be needed but as time goes on, healthier people means a smaller budget long term. A large chunk of the NHS budget is going straight to pharmaceutical companies.

Most of the drugs we need for crisis and emergency care exist already (and are off label) – pharmaceutical companies are clutching at straws to keep their business model alive. They are not interested in developing useful medication of short duration like a new antibiotic; most of the pharmaceutical industry research of today is now focused on lifetime medication like statins because there is less profit to be made in sickness and symptoms than there is in wellness. And that, ladies and gentlemen is the system our taxes is supporting.

My experience

Here is an extract from my first book, which I was inspired to write after my experience of the current healthcare model when I was suffering with appendicitis:

I found that they were only interested in the shortest way to alleviating my symptoms which was to douse me in strong medication, regardless of their side effects, and remove my appendix without consideration of the cost to my long-term health.

I understand emergency care is paramount, but I felt they lacked individuality to my case. Once it was clear my life wasn't in danger, other factors could be considered earlier such as my age, fitness levels, diet and emotional health. These were important factors that could have made my prognosis specific to me. At no point did anyone ask me for these metrics other than my age.

I was not asked if any personal triggers could have been a factor in my illness, neither was I asked about my diet to understand if I was nutrient deficient. There was no investigation into the cause of my inflamed appendix. The long-term risks of taking antibiotics were never mentioned nor any risks involved with the removal of my appendix.

The doctor's recommendation was to have my appendix removed, which would have undoubtedly relieved the symptoms – problem solved. Only I would have been left with fewer organs than I walked in with and more importantly, the underlying source of the issue was not considered, investigated, or addressed. Whilst my body was trying to tell me something, I was being viewed and assessed only by mechanistic measurements and solutions.

A brave new healthcare system

If we start with the end in mind, what would a perfect healthcare system look like? Hopefully we can all agree that in its current form there is room for improvement. The perfect healthcare system in my opinion would be with a proactive, cause-focused and patient-centred model with a holistic approach.

At some point in our lives everyone will need to access the healthcare system, even if we have been healthy throughout our lifetime; health is a time-limited blessing. One day we will age and develop health issues that will result in death. Healthcare needs to make the paradigm shift from focusing on the tail end of our life and spread healthcare over a lifetime, in my opinion.

By this, I mean periodically testing bloods, checking postural alignment, encouraging daily exercise, giving dietary advice and accepting that beliefs and emotions affect our health. With these markers, how many diseases could be prevented? We also need to educate student doctors and our nurses on the effect of our psychology has on our health.

Teach them that someone's thoughts and feelings could be the cause of their illness. Teach them the sickness timeline from psychological dis-ease to disease. Teach them about alternative therapies as well as pharmaceutical medication. In my mind the only reason this isn't happening now is because healthcare is a publicly funded and those funds are being manipulated by big business.

Introduction to the Hybrid Practitioner

In the future there won't be chiropractors, osteopaths, physiotherapists or even GPs; there will be Hybrid Practitioners and they will be part physician and part psychologist. Instead of going to see a practitioner to manage your symptoms, the Hybrid Practitioner will guide you through the cause of your symptoms, resolve emotional imbalances and be a mindset coach. Then and only then will they resort to other interventions, if symptoms do not resolve.

Attributes of Hybrid Practitioners

Not only will Hybrid Practitioners be specialists, they will take a holistic overview, tracing the cause back to its origin. At present within the medical model, someone with shoulder pain will only see a shoulder specialist; ask them about a knee and they will say 'I don't do knees'. Whereas the Hybrid Practitioner will include an assessment of an injured shoulder and they will also consider other possible causes, such as physical, mental and emotion onset.

Pain is informative for the Hybrid Practitioner, whereas the current healthcare model views pain as a problem that needs to be eradicated at all costs. The Hybrid Practitioner understands pain is a signal letting us know there is a problem. Painkillers can be useful in acute stages but they do not address the cause; a Hybrid Practitioner will focus a treatment plan and recommendations on a cure for the problem, instead of managing symptoms.

The hybrid practitioner would provide triage for patients with or without symptoms to direct them to whatever therapy would address their individual needs, in their opinion. They would be able to access diagnostic testing, such as bloods, stool and urine samples, MRIs and X-rays, to recommend the best treatment plan to suit that person. Specialists with a holistic mindset would be available to the triage work of other Hybrid Practitioners. Medication would be a last resort instead of an immediate go-to.

The evidence-based healer

The Hybrid Practitioner will possess many qualities and skills; however, the overarching concept is the role of the healer. Their ability to connect with their patients with empathy encourages and enhances the healing process, and remember *heal* is the first four letters of the word *health*. It won't matter what discipline or specialization they study or technique they practise – empathy is a quality that will be honed by the Hybrid Practitioner.

This is backed up by research; Practitioner's expressing empathy with patients, means the patient heals quicker and is more likely to take responsibility for their health in future, than practitioners than with less empathy. The placebo effect is when a person believes they can heal and is more likely to heal because they believe so, even in spite of a sham intervention. This is so reliable that a split tested random controlled trial, with an actual drug and a fake sugar pill, is the gold standard in the medical model. If people believe the sugar pill is the drug they are more likely to perceive the benefits of the actual drug, without taking the actual drug.

I've seen this in my own career as a practitioner. I've met physiotherapists, osteopaths and fellow chiropractors with a mindset not suited to the healer role and in my experience they will always struggle to connect with the patient emotionally, beyond reason, therefore limiting their results. The best practitioners I have met always knew the problem on the surface was just the symptom. They were able to touch the part of a person's psychology that would allow them to heal the cause, not only physically but also emotionally.

Kinesiology

A staple of a Hybrid Practitioner's assessment is to use kinesiology to find the cause diagnosis by muscle testing. Kinesiology testing is a precise science that connects to the body's innate intelligence, tapping into the deeper, subconscious part of us that is unfiltered and is a better judge of what we need than our filtered conscious mind.

This has been very useful in my own career as on many occasions I've found the problem is people are disconnected from their innate intelligence because they are locked into a filter (unconscious filters explain page XXX). I use kinesiology testing before any treatment takes place, whether large or small. I run all my diagnostics and treatment plans through these tests so that my professional opinion matches the patient's intuition.

Teaching the patient about body sense can be done through kinesiology testing. This will help them distinguish between their filters and their bodily intuition. This subtle skill is more powerful than anything else that be prescribed because this is a conversation with your own body.

Keep the faith

I know there are a questionable faith healers but I can't help be impressed by watching someone that's been in wheelchair for years suddenly stand and walk around on the command of a preacher. The person in a wheelchair defies reason because someone is telling them they can stand. The preacher tells us he is channelling a higher power that is supposedly telling them that this person can stand. A shift in this person's psychology motivates them to stand and they are willing to go through pain and disability to stand, taking their loved ones by surprise, as they also didn't believe this to be possible.

Regardless of whether you believe the preacher is channelling a higher power, they are definitely tapping into a person's beliefs that compel them emotionally to do the extraordinary. There is a common understanding in sales that people buy on emotion and then back their decisions up with reason.

The preacher doesn't whisper in their ear,with uncertainty and say 'I reckon you could stand' – he bellows this through a microphone in an auditorium full of believers, encouraging the audience into a belief structure of 'unreasonable' behaviour. Reasoning was never going to shift this person into believing they could stand, but healing them emotionally will and does.

There is a lot of cynicism towards faith healing and some is justified; however, by treating faith healing as folly because of the misuse by a few, we are throwing the baby out with the bath water. If we could ethically use faith healing in a professional, practitioner setting, not just for a freak show for monetary gain, we could maximize the healing potential for a patient's long-term best interests. If a practitioner had a model for tapping into the patient's psyche, to shift their beliefs, imagine the type of healthcare possible.

Healers can balance reason and emotion; this understanding of duality makes for excellent consols and leaders. They can bridge people's attitudes and ideas without landing on absolute or polar views or straw man arguments because they are tolerant, forgiving and kind. Natural healers are generally very earthy people, being in tune with natural laws of Beingism (see chapter one). They value honesty and for this reason can easily be overlooked by those that are not so inclined to do so.

The Hybrid Practitioner will play an important role but so will the patient. The practitioner will only be able to help a patient if they help themselves first. They can only take the patient as far as they are willing to go. A patient's recovery and long-term health is governed by the patient's belief structure, filters and management of their emotions.

A Hybrid Practitioner will know this and will be ready to assist the patient when they are ready to make changes. They will be listening for change talk from their patient such as 'I could do that' and then helping them structure those feelings into a plan of action, following the sage words of when the student is ready to learn the teacher will appear. They will be humanist practitioners, equal to the patients, encouraging education and *advising* instead of telling them and being authoritative experts such as now in the current healthcare model.

Pharmaceutical Healthcare	Hybrid Healthcare
Fixed labels and diagnosis Use a patented solution Patient dependence	Fluid label and diagnosis Resolve by addressing the cause Patient independence

The Hybrid Practitioner's stages for lifetime musculoskeletal health and wellness

This is a patient assessment I designed to help people become progressively more active without risk to further injury. Someone nursing an injury will need different exercise advice compared with someone without; therefore they would start in the first stage, which is to encourage healing only.

Once the injury has healed they can begin a remedial exercise phase which leads into a regular exercise. The last stage is all the benefits regular exercise gives us long term, which results in a new mindset connecting you with your life purpose.

Pain! (musculoskeletal)

Most people only seek care when pain is stopping them from a task they could do previously. In this stage the Hybrid Practitioner recommends treatment only, as your body needs healing and not remedial exercise. If you want to continue exercise, follow the rule: if a particular exercise aggregates then you must stop. Remember pain is informative to the Hybrid Practitioner and not something that needs eradicating, and it is resolved by addressing the cause and encouraging your body's natural healing response. The severity of the injury will dictate the time of recovery; either way the fastest recovery will be with treatment that enables innate healing and rest.

I recommend during this stage if there is pain, acute or

chronic, to use an ice protocol for the inflamed area, to aid and support the healing process. If you are suffering with pain at night I recommend this before bedtime and this can be done every 4-6 hours. If there is still a pain after this process, then this is when to escalate to over-the-counter medication (anti-inflammatory).

I never recommend over-the-counter (OTC) medication before an ice protocol for acute musculoskeletal pain. The body produces inflammation for a reason, to aid healing. OTC medication is designed to reduce and mask the pain – although at times reducing inflammation can be useful, this medication does not support the actual healing process, compared to the aforementioned ice protocol. Ice will help fresh blood flow to the area flush out old inflammation. (recap inflammatory response page XXX)

When someone stands from a chair and they need time to stand upright or they feel stiff or pain, this is a crisis injury in waiting; now is the time to act and resolve this issue. The signs are already there that a restriction is in place; when the injury comes, this will be the tip of the iceberg. We are conditioned to believe this is just old age; we soldier on and the longer we continue to ignore the warning signs the stiffer we will become and the more likely we will feel a protective muscle spasm (musculoskeletal pain). The time to address this stiffness and pain is now, not when you are so bad that you cannot get off the floor because of pain.

Remedial exercise

Let's define what we mean by remedial exercise. If a person's range of joint motion is sufficient and the muscles supporting the joint are strong, there will be no need to do remedial exercises. You could run, jump, do push-ups, lunges and squats. However, for most people, certainly those with sedentary lifestyles, often their joints are stiff from a lack of activity and the lack of appropriate exercise to strengthen them.

It's a common tale of how someone will injure themselves after a period of inactivity – they go straight back into a strength or high-volume training program and they pull a muscle or their 'back goes'. They had done a similar exercise program before and they thought they could pick up from where they left off. However, in that time their muscles had lost their tone, and their balance and coordination had diminished, resulting in a susceptibility to injury.

A remedial pathway is about restoring the range of motion in the joint and setting up the person so they can progress back to fully functioning with the minimum risk to injury. Once they are fully functioning, remedial exercises become their warm-up and cool-down protocol because these exercises encourage good movement and posture. They are mostly fully functional exercises broken into smaller movements so that they can be achieved with a view to include the other parts in time.

Fully functioning

When niggling injuries are resolved and good postural alignment is corrected, risk of injury relapse is less likely; therefore restoring normal movement patterns and increasing repetition can be done safely. This means being able to move, bend, twist or pick an object up from the floor without pain or fear of pain. Similar to the remedial phase, fully functioning is a progressive state and as time goes on it not only maintains but continues to improve posture and movement.

With the guidance of a Hybrid Practitioner someone can take more responsibility for their long-term health by entering into a functional exercise program with weights or body weight only. Just performing function movements regularly, with good form and an understanding of your joints, is what is going to make you healthy, with the added bonus of preventing disease and **all-cause mortality**.

If someone is exercising and is experiencing pain or discomfort, before or after, I would suggest dropping into a remedial phase or posture-change program before the injury worsens or creates compensatory injuries. Muscular niggles are caused because a muscle or joint is under more pressure than nature intends when moving or during exercise; they are paying the sins of another restricted joint or poor movement pattern. If we continue to ignore the warning signs, without addressing the issue, we risk a more serious injury in the future.

Being able to maintain the fully functioning state will reflect in your personality, making you able to be stoic regarding situations and fulfilling your ambitions, but also humble enough to still care about others.

This is the formula to maintaining excellent health throughout a lifetime. Many make the mistake of stopping exercise after the remedial phase; they reach a plateau and risk the problem returning. How many people do you know that are still doing the same physiotherapy exercises year after year? Fully functioning is about going past that point to enter a new phase, in the sense that the original issue has resolved and this is maintained and progressed through a functional program.

Self-actualization

This is where the limiting conditioning of modern medicine is broken. Once progressing in the fully functioning state for at least a year, people realize that pain is not just a must that happens as we age and is more because we become stagnant to proper and correct movement. The reason this phase takes at least a year is because you need to experience health through a fully functioning body that is exercising regularly. We feel good after workouts in the short term and this good feeling compounds as our body becomes healthier and stronger. The sage advice of healthy body, healthy mind matches us with our purpose.

By living a fully functioning lifestyle, people are taking responsibility and they understand health comes from within and not from a prescribed medication. Fully functioning is about restoring health and moving well; self-actualization is a lifetime mindset towards a chosen path of purpose, principle and meaning.

A self-actualized mindset is living a life with a set of values and principles (beliefs) that make sense to that person. It's about being tolerant, forgiving of themselves and others so that lessons can be learnt, instead of blaming others, and this unresolved resentment ripples out into future generations. A self-actualized person, even when triggered by events, will be proactive in their manner, to process their emotions and when appropriate they will reflect and refine their own behaviour without losing the value of that behaviour.

This mindset is the tip of the iceberg to living an active lifestyle through regular exercise or sport, eating a balanced diet, living in moderation as opposed to abstinence. This mindset will consider life as a miracle, leaning towards a belief in a universal higher power. They will be philosophical about the past, with an attitude of what's meant to be will be and that everything happens for a reason, acknowledging signs of synchronicity and coincidence. When the mental, emotional, physical and spiritual states combine, this is self-actualizing.

This is where our power is. A self-actualized individual will begin to dream of a future that people conditioned by the limiting beliefs of the current healthcare model could never dream of. They will rise above limiting beliefs to self-actualize a life in alignment with themselves and those close to them, nurturing a state of inner peace. Life starts to become less about their problems and more about viewing them as a blessing.

This is where Stoical Beingism as a philosophy can be practised and honed to suit your own personal circumstances. You will break out of the apathy of choosing what advertiser put in front of us or questionable push messages by governments, and make your own choices. At this stage I encourage people to develop their own principles and values that make sense to them, so they are in alignment with themselves. In my experience going through these phases, building a physical foundation to maintain abstract values and principles, leads to a self-actualized life. As mentioned earlier a healthy body and a healthy mind are a reflection of each other.

Olympic athletes are typically self-actualized individuals, gifted but also dedicated in their craft, supported by a self-belief mindset and routine. These athletes are humble in victory and quick to credit their coaches or team for their success. They will be stoic in defeat by congratulating their opponents on their win and they usually vow to learn from their losses.

Muhammad Ali, aka Cassius Clay, is a real-life example of a self-actualized person. He was a supremely gifted athlete, with a mesmerizing speed of movement and personality to match. He was also dedicated to his sport, he was known for pushing himself in training and would rise early morning to go for a run; even when he had progressive Parkinson's, he still rose in the early hours to pray till the day he died.

He lived life on his terms, standing up for what he believed, staying true his own code and values regardless of the consequences. Ali threw his Olympic gold medal into the Ohio River, after being chased by a gang on his return from the Olympic Games held in Rome in 1962. He made a vow to himself that night he wasn't going to be who they wanted him to be – he was going to be who he wanted to be. This was a troubling time in America during the civil rights movement and Ali was prepared to go against the grain in order to live in accordance with his own principles.

In 1968 his anti-establishment position came to a head, when the government stripped him of his heavyweight title and boxing licence as a punishment for not enlisting in the army for the Vietnam War. Ali was famous for saying at the time, 'I ain't got no quarrel with them Viet Cong'. This made him unpopular and he was portrayed as unpatriotic and a coward. Ali maintained his reasons, standing by them against the unjust system of segregation and in supported of the civil rights movement.

The Ali story doesn't end there and amongst his vast number of achievements he would be vindicated for his position by posterity; he was also voted the greatest athlete of the 20th century and he lit the flame at the Atlanta games in 1996. His life is one of principles and values. Self-actualizing isn't about being popular, although that's not to say you won't be; it's about making a stand and being respectful of others' stand. He was prepared to give up his career for his principles and the world is better place for his sacrifices.

Ali was a special person and although many of us won't be put in a position of needing to make the sacrifices he did, we can live a life of principles regardless of our circumstances. If more people made a stand for what they believed, how big or small is irreverent, we all play our part in creating this shared world.

Anyone can reach self-actualization – by going through the wellness stages, this will be more attainable to you. I can describe it but no one can tell you what self-actualizing is – you must experience it for yourself. The opposite is living the life of the eternal victim, being thought controlled, not helping yourself and then blaming others without being solution focused.

I would suggest that anyone yo-yoing with their weight, taking a collection of pills without attempting other conservative, holistic treatments beforehand or feeling stuck physically mentally and emotionally in their life is not not self-actualizing.

People can make a decision to change their mindset overnight, but the road to self-actualizing isn't an overnight journey; they will need to go through many iterations and challenges, with a consistent approach over a period of time, to develop new beliefs and behavioural patterns to raise their game of life.

Summary

Our current healthcare model is collapsing and has a record-breaking waiting list for non-life-threatening surgeries and procedures. I hope from reading this chapter it's clear to see the healthcare model currently employed is outdated and antiquated. Healthcare needs to change to support life forces as prevention and not only when they break down. This shift will happen – it is only a matter of time – and we can either plan this shift in advance or wait until a complete collapse of the current model. We are delaying because of big business and its stranglehold over healthcare policy.

The Hybrid Practitioner is a solution to these healthcare problems. They understand that healing is a powerful treatment in conjunction with other treatments. They will help their patients to think holistically and help them even before they are sick. They will heal their patient's physical, emotion and spiritual wounds, which will raise universal consciousness. A Hybrid Practitioner marks a shift in mindset that will revolutionize healthcare at no extra cost.

Healthcare systems quiz

1) Healthcare at present is
a) Proactive
b) Reactive
c) Holistic
d) Having a capacity to acknowledge psychological dis-ease

2) Pain is?
e) A feeling that needs to be eradicated at all costs
f) Information to let us know there is a problem
g) To be ignored
h) An absolute consequence of advancement in age

3) A Hybrid Practitioner...
a) Is only interested in your symptoms
b) Will only wait until you are sick before acknowledging your concerns
c) Is cause focused of symptoms
d) Thinks a holistic approach is nonsense

4) A holistic healthcare system would in the long term?
a) Be cost prohibitive
b) Be a waste of time
c) Make people unhealthier
d) Save money

5) Empathy has the ability to do what to the healing process?
a) Slow down healing
b) Speed up healing
c) Has no effect on healing
d) Is harmful to the healing process

6) Healthy broken into heal-thy means?

a) You heal
b) You heel
c) Has no meaning and is a coincidence
d) Medication is needed

7) Kinesiology is?

a) Voodoo
b) A scientifically proven way to test muscle
c) Magic
d) An unproven muscle test

8) The goal of a Hybrid Practitioner for their patient is?

a) Manage their pain
b) Self actualize an independent lifestyle
c) Medicate before using other interventions
d) Make them dependant on them

9) The placebo effect is

a) A non-belief
b) A measure only useful in drug trials
c) A belief
d) Mystical and magical

Practical physical education

While you are changing into your gym clothes I will explain today's physical education lesson. In school PE revolves around the rules, technique and the playing of sport. In the Back Doctor School of Health, PPE (practical physical education) is learning how our bodies move so that if we are inclined to play sport or partake in regular exercise, we will be better at them and will be less susceptible to injury, and if injury occurs we know how to manage it.

This chapter is again challenging the apathy of believing that as we age, we will feel pain more often as an absolute consequence of the advancement of age. The ageing process is a factor to consider, but musculoskeletal pain at any age can be resolved or lessened by partaking in a progressive exercise program designed to restore good movement and function. This chapter is broken into examples of remedial exercise for hip and lower back, shoulder and neck, to being fully functioning (exercising in general). There will be advice on typical general exercise, common complaints and advice on self-help when injured.

The **outside-in** approach encourages us to wait for our health to decline before taking action, which is an antiquated model of healthcare and not in your best interest. Our lifelong medication starts now, by beginning an exercise program within our limits, with a view to progressing to a fully functioning and a self-actualizing lifestyle. If a person is suffering with joint pain, there is a more than good chance that a remedial exercise program will improve or resolve this pain.

Benefits of exercise

You can believe in this: regular exercise is scientifically proven to improve your life expectancy, self-esteem, depression, concentration levels, short- and long-term memory, successful career progression and many other benefits. When we exercise regularly within our limits there seems to be no downside.

Exercise is proven to reduce **all-cause mortality** and will not only prevent diseases, it will also slow the progression of them. As little as 30 minutes of walking multiple times a week is all that is needed to unlock these health benefits. Exercising within your limits is also an excellent way to manage chronic pain syndromes, maintain a healthy weight and acts as a stress reliever. Weight-bearing exercise is the number one recommendation to osteoporosis sufferers because using body weight on the bones increases the bone mass which has been lost.

Examples of <u>all cause mortality</u> which regular exercise will not only help to prevent but will also slow the progression of these diseases

Regular exercise will make you feel good and is also good for your health, so if you're quite finished changing, let's head outside...

Benefits of sunlight

Not only does sunlight feel good but the Sun's rays have a range of health benefits such as keeping our bones strong. When partaking in exercise, being outdoors is an easy way to acquire vitamin D, which our bodies generate from exposure to sunlight. It is fantastic for people with underlying health issues and can help those advanced in years slow the ageing process. Sunlight is known to be a germicide from its ultraviolet light, therefore slowing the transmission of infections.

Benefits of fresh air

Fresh air also has many health benefits. Walks in nature, away from congested areas and pollution, are great for our cardiovascular system. Breathing in fresh air is proven to be healthy for us and, again, it provides an excuse to be outside. The effect of congested air is seen by children living in urban areas, as they are more likely to be asthmatic than children living in less built-up ones.

Finding your baseline and entry-level fitness

Starting a fitness program is good for you but not all exercise is good for everyone. For example, if your body has restricted movement to protect acute (fresh) inflammation at a joint (explained in the microbiology chapter XXX), a high-impact exercise program, with a high volume of repetition, such as running or HIT training will risk a higher chance of injury, especially if the warning signs (the injury site) are already present. This chapter offers a template for most baseline fitness and for people returning from injury to progress on their fitness journey.

General exercise and daily living

Walking

Walking is the easiest and safest place to start on the commencement of any exercise program, as walking has low impact on our joints. This means that with each step there is minimal force, unlike running which out the force of up to 12 times your body weight on each foot on impact. A common issue when walking after a period of time is a person's back begins to hurt. A likely cause is postural restrictions within the hips and lower back causing a suboptimal and asymmetrical gait.

When the hip and lower back are restricted they will eventually lead to issues with foot mechanics causing plantar fasciitis, morton's neuroma, calluses or bunions. In my model the solution is to free the restriction in the hip and lower back and then the foot will recover quickly, instead of using an orthotic insert in the shoe. Orthotics can be useful but they can be overprescribed by practitioners and relied upon by the patient too readily in my opinion. Think of the toes like piano keys: when the keys are played, a cord is pulled and on the end of this cord is a hammer deep in the piano, which hits the note. The hip muscles are the hammer and if the cord to the hammer is too tight or loose it will affect he sound of the note. If the hip muscles are restricted, the toes and feet pay the sins of those restrictions in the hip.

The principle of good walking is easy to remember because it is the same for maintaining good posture from the side. When we step out, instead of lunging forward with a large step we want to keep the knee, hip, shoulder and head stacked on top of each other. This means a shorter step but a more upright posture, allowing a heel strike and the foot to roll through onto the forefoot. This upright posture when walking initiates the core, buttocks and other postural muscles of the spine. Over striding will activate the hip flexors, instead of synchronizing with the postural muscles. When the spine loses its stacked posture, the postural muscles cannot support the spine; only the heel strikes and the foot doesn't go though the full step, which is what causes foot problems.

Cycling

The easiest step up from walking to improve cardiovascular fitness, while maintaining a low impact, is cycling. Most people at some point in their life learn how to ride a bicycle and many of us own one in the garden shed. Using a racer or a mountain bike is great start for people returning to fitness, fresh air and exploring. To improve cardiovascular fitness we need to maintain a high heart rate during the exercise (depending on your age, that high heart rate zone will differ).

For those returning from injury the bike provides a low-impact alternative to running. I personally take a long ride once a week on my mountain bike across the countryside and ride to the gym as a warm-up. I keep the bike in a high gear, using it like a fixed gear bike, to increase the level of difficulty, which raises my pulse and strengthens my legs and upper body muscles. It might surprise you that when riding we are working our upper body muscles, as they are working in unison with our legs. Our upper body and core muscles steady the bike for the legs to drive through the pedals.

Sitting

Sitting for short periods is fine but **prolonged bouts of sitting consistently day after day are as bad for our health as smoking,** the reason being is that nature intended you to move and stand while being upright and symmetrical. When we sit for prolonged periods our natural posture deteriorates because our centre of gravity changes from the belly button to being level with the heart. This means our upper body is placing more stress on certain discs of the spine, rather than evenly distributing over many discs.

Over time our postural muscles adapt to these new positions, which can cause tension-based headaches, a forward head posture, rounded shoulders, weakened buttock muscles and shortening of our hip flexors, which leads to increased likelihood of chronic pain and increased risk of injuries from day-to-day activities and playing sport. Physical pain is the least of our worries as prolonged sitting increases the risks of heart disease, diabetes, metabolic syndrome, cancer and a shorter life span.

We live in a culture in the Western world where we sit and we do the worst kind of sitting, right angled at the hips and putting weight onto our hamstrings. We sit when we put our socks on the morning, when we eat a meal, when we drive or when we use a computer. The Japanese live longer than any other culture and the general agreed theory is because of their diet and mindset but their culture also encourages floor living. This means that when they sit they either kneel or are on the floor and are able to rise from the floor again with ease.

I recommend maintaining your ability to do this by each morning putting your socks on while sitting on the floor, in doing so maintain and assessing your movement function daily. If this is difficult to do then I suggest seeking out a practitioner because this is an injury in waiting. The incidence of falls is a major cause of declining health in the elderly, and is higher, with a slower recovery rate, in the Western world compared to the Eastern. Being able to maintain the ability to go to the floor and rise again will help prevent falls in the elderly.

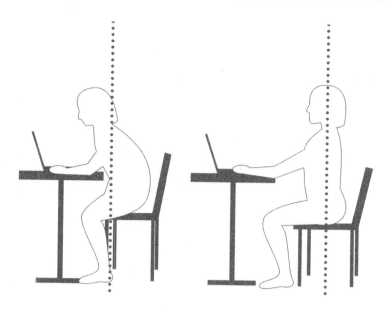

If you are in this category of people who are sitting for more than eight hours, day after day, then there is hope, because not all sitting is created equal. There are some changes to our sitting posture that can be immediately implemented to reduce some of the effects of sitting. Instead of sitting on your hamstrings, bring your bum close to the edge of the seat and sit on the part of the pelvis commonly known as the sitting bones. Use squat principles (page XXX) by placing your feet more than shoulder width apart, arching the feet and pushing your knees outward. In this position the spine and postural muscles are less likely to slouch.

Standing

As mentioned, I don't recommend prolonged sitting and instead encourage my office-based patients, once their posture been corrected, to stand for a portion of the day. Standing is natural for us when compared to sitting in right-angled chairs, which was only invented in the last thousand or so years. When standing with correct posture our centre of gravity is close to the pelvis and our body will be upright.

Standing engages the postural muscles that support the spine, the traps, erector spines, quadratus lumborum (QL), abdominal core and the buttocks. Using these muscles regularly engages them to maintain an upright posture. Whereas **prolonged sitting** turns off these muscles groups and encourages poor postural alignment such as forward head posture and rounded shoulders, placing a counter lever on the lower back muscles and spinal joints.

When we stand we are removing the biggest trigger of lower back pain, neck pain and shoulder pain, **prolonged sitting**. Standing also burns more calories than sitting; therefore we are more likely to lose weight as a result. Your legs have the biggest muscles groups in the body but many of us are not using their potential.

When people start standing at work they become tired quickly for this reason. There is a knack to standing for prolonged periods. I advise when starting to stand to take regular breaks by sitting in the way I described above; this will gradually build endurance in our legs. When standing I advise you to shift the weight occasionally from one leg to another, use a foot stool and perch on the edge of a stool. Movement is encouraged when standing. Once the strength improves in our legs, standing will feel easier.

A remedial exercise that is good for learning how to connect with your postural muscles is to stand with your feet straight and clench your buttock muscles, letting your knees rotate outwards and the feet arch. Then retract your shoulders while maintaining your core muscles so that your back does not over-arch. Imagine zipping up a jacket with your core muscles from your navel to the bottom of your sternum. Hold this for 10 seconds and then release. This is same form as holding the plank position (page XXX) but in a standing position.

This will also benefit any exercise that uses the buttocks such as the bridge and core-based exercises. The plank, which is both a remedial and fully functioning exercise, is excellent for syncing up the shoulder with your core and buttocks.

Pushing activities (such as hoovering)

Hoovering, pushing a trolley or pram or lawn mowing are common triggers mentioned when people are suffering with back pain; therefore I will offer advice on this sort of task. When you lose the shape of your spine, even if in a resting posture, you are more susceptible to neck and lower back issues; combining that with poor form when loading and generating force is a recipe for backache.

When patients tell me they feel pain when they do pushing activities, I usually ask them to demonstrate how they use, for example, the hoover. They normally put both feet together, hingeing at the hips and leaning their upper body over their toes, with knees straight, outstretching their arms in a back or forth motion. This position is a compromised position for our lower back and pain will happen sooner rather than later.

The solution is to place your feet in a boxing or karate stance, with the arm of the opposite foot forward, holding the hoover (the same whether for a hose or upright hover). This stance allows movement at our knees to dip instead of hingeing with straight legs and leaning forward. Secondly the arms move but they do not move outside of our core control. Imagine there is a half moon circle of approximately 30 centimetres to our front and this is the limit that our arms will go and not beyond. To go further we move our feet closer to the object area.

By not overextending the arms and leaning forward, our feet move position and the knees bend, therefore our back remains upright. Instead of overreaching with our arms and hingeing at the hips, our back maintains being straight and upright. The same formula is used for any task that involves pushing or pulling, as with a pram or trolley.

Good form when hoovering = less likelihood of lower back pain.

This position causes counter lever on the lower back = more likelihood of lower back pain

Sleeping

Always sleep where possible with good ventilation and avoid digital light before bedtime. The blue light of digital devices stops the release of melatonin, which is a chemical released in the brain to aid sleep. This is related to the body's clock known as the circadian rhythm, which releases chemicals throughout the day and especially at night time. Digital light tricks the internal body clock into thinking its daytime and therefore it doesn't release melatonin at bedtime. This will negatively affect the quality of sleep, which is needed to be healthy.

Quality sleep is as significant as eating a healthy diet and taking exercise. When we sleep our body repairs, therefore if our sleep is being affected this will eventually fatigue our daytime posture and negatively affect our health, similar to that of being stuck in fight or flight. Our body's energy and resources are not unlimited and they need to be recharged by sleep and a better quality of sleep means better health and function.

I get asked a lot about what pillow I recommend or what bed will solve someone's back pain. My first recommendation is always to correct your postural alignment before even considering what pillow or bed you are using. If you are feeling pain at night, the pillow or the bed might be contributing to your current pain, but this was never the cause – the development of poor posture is. When patients still focus on the bed or the pillow as a cause after multiple explanations, this in many cases is a telltale sign of an outside-in mindset. I encouraging changing this mindset as a higher priority than making an investment in a new bed or pillow.

I recommend sleeping with one pillow that can be folded underneath when lying on your side. The height of the pillow needs to change as we roll because when we are on our back, the head is only raised slightly above our shoulders, compared to side lying; but when we are lying on our side the height needs to match the elevation of the raised head because of the shoulder.

If I recommend a bed I prefer a firmer mattress over a soft one. Again a person's posture and preferences will dictate whether they need a soft or a firm mattress. I find that the better someone's posture is, the more likely a firmer mattress will be OK for that person.

A common trigger for problems is sitting up in bed. The reason is similar to other sitting: postural muscles are unable to provide stability because of the hinge at the hips and rounding of the back on the soft base of the mattress. By bending the knees or placing a pillow underneath, this will minimize the hip hinge. Next is to avoid rounding your back and this can done by lying flat and propping your head upright, so there is a straight line between shoulder and hip. This means the neck is supported and the back remains straight and not rounding. This is suitable for reading a book or watching TV.

Gardening

There are many different positions that come under the heading of gardening, such as bending, twisting and lifting. The general rule for gardening is the same for most other activities, to keep your back straight, using squatting and the dead lift technique when lifting (page XXX) and if you do need to round your back because of an awkward position, be aware not to lift anything unreasonably heavy on your own that could send your back into a protective spasm. Judge the difference between a one-person lift and a two-person lift.

Limit bending time by kneeling on a single knee or both and use a cushion to soften the pressure on the knees. This is also a good position to pick up objects instead of bending with straight legs to the floor. A classic gardening trigger is pulling weeds out of the ground, hingeing at the hips with straight knees. This is the worst position for our back and hips as our postural muscles are not able to provide stability much in the same way as overreaching with straight legs when hoovering.

With one knee on the floor the counter lever is reduced through the lower back, and keeping our back straight and stable is more manageable. Rounding our back isn't the issue, rounding with a counter lever weight too many times without support is. When pain happens it's usually the tip of an iceberg of warning signs of improper and restrictive movement.

Good form when
lifting: this uses
your core muscles
protecting your
back

Poor form lifting:
This rounds the
back causing a
counter lever

Physical self-help manual
for musculoskeletal issues when exercising

Trigger point therapy

Identifying areas of restriction is the first step to resolving improper movement, which is the likely cause of niggling injuries or the susceptibility to them. Muscles are interconnected fibres that pull together to move joints; when they are healthy they will move our joints through their full range of motion. When those fibres are used repetitively and incorrectly, they increase the likelihood of those muscles becoming 'knotted', reducing the range of motion, therefore also not providing the movement and function nature intended.

Sure signs of when a joint or muscle is knotted are that it will stiffen more than usual, pain might be present when exercising, or it will be tender to touch because inflammation is in the joints afterwards or constantly. When people use the word 'knotted' to describe a muscle, what they mean is the muscle is currently injured or the injury has healed with scar tissue, causing a tough fibrous lump in the muscles that can be felt on the skin. These are known as trigger points; they are tender and fibrous because they are taking more strain than the other parts of the muscle, due to improper movement at the joint.

It's best to address the cause of the injury by viewing the patient holistically to resolve the problem long term, but in the short term these 'knots' within muscles will benefit from direct pressure and friction on the trigger point or scar tissue. Moving the joint at the same time as applying pressure can help to restore the range of the joint and break down scar tissue further, which is the likely reason for restriction of the joint.

Massage therapy is based around this premise of finding the 'knots' of trigger points or scar tissue build-ups and then using friction and pressure to break them down. A massage therapist will spend time warming up muscles and joints and then they will usually focus their pressure on those areas of knotty trigger points and scar tissue. I recommend massage. I also recommend learning how to self-treat trigger points. Above all I recommend learning to improve your movement so that you can prevent knots from happening in the first place.

Foam rolling

One tool used for self-trigger pointing is a foam roller which is a low cost, storable piece of equipment. Think of a foam roller as a human rolling pin that targets trigger points and scar tissue, so that the muscles can move their fibres in the intended direction and improve the joint's range of motion. This can be used before or after exercise, improving performance and maintaining joint health.

If in doubt I invite you to do this test to demonstrate the power of using a foam roller. Stand in front of a mirror or film yourself doing a squat. Now use the foam roller for 10 minutes, focusing the pressure on areas of the legs and the sticky painful areas in your buttocks, hamstrings, quads, and calf muscles. Once this has been done, please return to the mirror or re-film yourself and compare the difference. Usually the feel of the squat will be easier, and your butt will be closer to the ground and more symmetrical than the first time. You will feel less stiff and more comfortable during the execution of the squat.

With practice and understanding how the muscles' fibres work, using a self-trigger point tool can be useful in managing injuries or when warming up and cooling down. Everyday objects can be used as well, such as a golf ball, hockey ball or tennis ball.

Hip flexers

Calves

ITB

Quads

Adductors

Buttocks

Upper body protocol

Remedial

External rotation of shoulders

When our spine loses the ability to be upright from the side, the ribcage tilts forward, and over time our shoulders will adapt and internally rotate inwards because of this. This is commonly known as rounded shoulders or having shoulders internally rotated, which means this person's shoulders are forward of their ideal position; the shoulder blade comes away from the spine and ribcage to the side of the body. The postural muscles of the mid back are lengthened and are unstable. Therefore they are unable to support the spine's upright posture, and not only does the spine lose the ideal position, this new position also puts more pressure on the spine.

The solution is to understand and encourage scapula retraction (pulling the shoulder blades back and down) when moving the shoulders. This means bracing the shoulders by squeezing the scapulas together downwards on your back. In this position the shoulders are stable and externally rotated, limiting the instability of internal rotation. By retracting the shoulders we are helping our spine be upright and reducing the forward tilt of the ribcage.

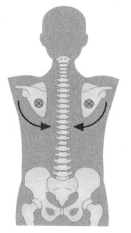 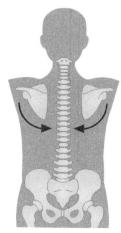

Waiter hands

A simple exercise to develop external rotation of your shoulders is relax your arms by your side and bend your forearms at a right angle. Then place your hands face up to the ceiling, imagining you're a waiter holding a plate in each hand. Notice that the scapula will naturally draw inward and downwards. I recommend learning to retract your scapula for shoulder, neck and ribcage misalignment.

1. Imagine screwing your scapula in to your back (scapula back and down)
2. Avoid raising your shoulders and engaging the upper traps
3. Hold for 10 seconds rest for 10 seconds

This is a daily remedial exercise to counteract the ribcage tilting forward, to retract a forward head posture and prevent a person's shoulders from rolling inward, which I recommend in conjunction with treatment. Treatment is vital because this will remove any jamming in the facet joints (bones of the spine that connect to the ribcage) which are causing the head and shoulder to come forward. Performing retracting shoulder exercises with treatment speeds up improvements because treatment will restore natural movements for the exercise to progress.

Once the person is in fully functioning phase, retraction exercises are still relevant and are best used before any functional shoulder movements. Scapula retraction is the cornerstone of any shoulder movement or exercise.

Once we understand scapula retraction we can then incorporate the arm. This is best done with isometric exercises to begin with to build up static strength but then bands and weights can be used. The plank is a good example of scapula retraction using the arm in an isometric exercise – see page XXX.

Straight arms from midline to cross position

Place straight arms out in front of you and touch the hands together – imagine they are in a closed clap. Remember to screw the shoulder blades, engage the core and buttocks and arch the feet, and bring your straight arms away from the midline until level with the body. While scapula retracting I would expect you to feel this between your shoulder blades and rotator cuff muscles. While maintaining that tension of scapula retraction (screwing shoulder blades), return straight arms to the closed clap position. Focus on form, perfecting the scapula retraction. Do this until fatigued and build up to 12–16 repetitions.

Bent arms from midline to W position

Place arms bent at the elbow in the midline so that the elbows and forearms are touching. Remember the cue to screw shoulder blades, engage core and buttocks and arch feet; bring bent arms away from one another till level with the body from the side. Again I would expect the muscles between the shoulder blades and rotator cuff muscles to be the area where you feel contraction. While maintaining the tension of scapula retraction, return the bent arms to the midline. Do to fatigue and build up to 12–16 reps.

Olympic shoulders

Scapula retract shoulders, then draw elbows downwards so that your forearms are horizontal to the ground and then attempt to flatten your hands, imagining there is plate on them. Hold for a few seconds, focusing on muscular contraction of scapula retraction, and avoid engaging the upper trap, which dominates over those smaller muscles groups underneath.

Shoulder fully functioning

Plank

I seldom recommend any core exercise like a traditional sit-up. People regularly exercising will be fine but for people with postural issues, doing crunching-type exercises is a potential risk for injury and could make current injuries worse.

Pilates-based exercises for beginners are best for those in need of postural changes before advancing. These are mostly small movement exercises, fine tuning muscles to fire core muscles in order to align pelvis, trunk and shoulders. They are excellent for encouraging posture change and one in particular is a staple, called the plank.

The plank doesn't look much but when done correctly all our postural muscles as mentioned earlier are being used. It's an isometric exercise, which means, instead of contracting muscles, the muscles used stay the same length. Notice in this position the back is not dropping below the pelvis so that there is no risk of the back being compromised; if the form is compromised or pain is felt, stop immediately or modify by placing your knees on the floor.

Lie on your front with arms outstretched, similar to a press-up position, or on your elbows in line with your shoulders. Lift the body onto the balls of your feet to make a straight line from your shoulder to the ankles, by squeezing your butt and leg muscles, core abdominal area and muscles between your shoulder blades, and hold this position. To modify this position, place your knees on the floor. This is a great exercise for stopping a forward head posture because of the strengthening and synchronization of the muscles of the pelvis, trunk and shoulders.

Press-ups

A press-up is similar to a plank with outstretched arms in the starting position. Instead of a static, isometric exercise, a press-up movement is bending arms to lower to the floor and extending to return to the original position, while maintaining an isometric tension within the core muscles and buttocks.

Adopt the plank position with hands on the floor and under the shoulders. Lower the body by letting the elbows go away from the body until the chest is one fist width from the floor. Stabilise scapula retraction for a moment and then begin the upward phase by allowing the scapulas to rotate outward to the side and the elbows to straighten.

To modify this exercise, again place the knees on the floor. Use a bolster under your chest to elevate the floor so that you break down the full movement further. Another tip is to press from a table to build strength gradually (see opposite).

It's is a fantastic exercise for upper body strength and also a core exercise too.

Lower body protocol

Remedial

Knees to chest

pic 25

Lie on your back with your feet on the floor and your knees bent. Bring both knees into your chest, wrap your arms around them and feel for the stretch across the lower back area, holding for 10 seconds. Roll to either side with lower back and hips at a right angle and keeping shoulders on the floor. Do the same with one knee into the chest; at the same time roll towards the opposite side to the knee into the chest.

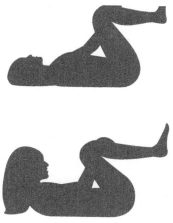

Bridge

Lie flat on your back with your knees bent and feet flat on the floor. Follow standing/squat teaching points (page XXX) and screw in the buttock muscles, removing any curve from the lower back and then drive your hips upwards using your buttocks. Hold for a few seconds before lowering; notice for any tightness, restrictions or weakness when performing the exercise.

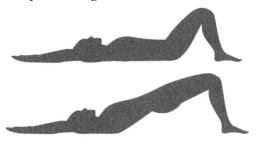

Buttock stretch lying flat on back

Lie on your back bending one knee on the floor and then with the other leg let the knee drop out to the side and rest the foot on the opposite knee. Pull the knee towards the chest, feeling for a muscle stretch deep in the buttock called the piriformis and push the knee away to feel a stretch in the side of the buttocks. What normally happens with people at the beginning of a posture change program is they will likely feel tightness on the opposite sides, due to their asymmetrical posture.

Rolling side to side lying flat on back

Lie with the foot resting on the knee and roll to either side to feel the stretch in different parts of the hip. When the knee goes to the opposite, across the body you'll likely feel it in the lateral buttocks and lower back and the knee on the same side. You will also feel it in the front of the opposite hip. If this is too much in the beginning bring the knees into the body and then drop them to either side.

Lower body fully functioning

Squatting and dead lifting

When people use the terms squatting and dead lifting they usually think of weight training; however, we are all performing these tasks to some degree more often than we realize. For instance, when we sit in a chair, this is the beginning of the squat and standing up is the return position. Or another example is when we pick something up from the floor regardless of the weight or form – this is a dead lift. Therefore if we are already doing these movements multiple times a day then we might as well learn to do them well.

The teaching points are the same as for the full squat:

1. Actively contract buttock muscles to pull outward and sideways
2. Do not let knee pass go over the toes
3. Arch foot and keep feet straight (if adductors are tight and the buttock muscles are weak the heels draw towards the midline)
4. A straight line will be present from your ear to hip.

Sitting to standing

Start by sitting on the edge of a seat so that the sitting bones are taking the weight; your back is straight with your feet shoulder width apart. To stand, engage the arches of your feet, push the weight onto the outside edges, and push knees outward too, without them going over toes. At the last portion of the upward phase squeeze your butt muscles.

Reverse the order on the way down, by hingeing at the hips, lowering them towards the chair. Hinge backwards at the hips to stop the knees from going in front of the toes. Again, activate the arches in your feet, preventing the knees from collapsing inward. Control the descent before placing your bottom back onto the edge of the chair. This exercise can be performed multiple times and I strongly recommend doing this any time you sit or rise from a chair.

Afghan squat

One way to improve your squatting is to practise the Afghan squat. If you read my first book I mentioned I went to Afghanistan as a Marine on a tour of duty. The Afghan culture is a beautiful thing to behold. They are humble, earthy people, connected to nature, and this showed in how they moved. I was surprised at first when I noticed they didn't use chairs; instead they would sit in a deep squat with ease for long periods that is virtually impossible for most of my new patients that enter our clinic. The benefits are backed by science because there is a lower incidence of lower back pain in cultures that squat as a sitting posture.

It's a really good stretch for the hips and the lower back muscles. Squat down all the way to the feet while maintaining both soles on the floor. This might take practice and in the beginning holding onto a support is needed until the joints open again and balance is assured.

The teaching points are the same as for the full squat:

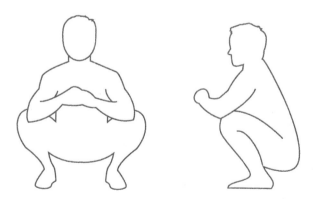

If Afghan squatting correctly, there will be no pain in the knees and there will likely be a stretch feeling across the lower back, buttocks and the inside of the thighs. When changing posture this is to be done daily for three times a day for three minutes. The regularity will increase the mobility of the hip joints that contribute to not only lower back issues but also neck and shoulders issues too. After doing this daily for a week or so finding balance without support becomes easier and there will be an increased feeling of strength and flexibility.

Once mobility has been achieved, full squats are more attainable with minimal risk to injury. Just as scapula retraction is a warm-up for shoulder exercises, Afghan squatting will become a warm-up to any squat and leg workout. This exercise is a progression to maintain the fully functioning state and that means moving and strengthening your joints through their full range of motion, regularly and often.

To test the effectiveness of the Afghan squat, bend forward from your hips and measure how close your hands are to your toes. Now perform the Afghan squat with your feet flat on the floor, feeling a stretch in your lower back and hips for a minute or so. Go back to standing and bending from your hips and see the difference. Without stretching the hamstrings you will feel more flexible bending forward. That's why stretching the hamstrings on their own is futile; they are tight because they are compensating for lack of mobility in the hips and lower back.

Lunge

Step forward or back a stride width while maintaining a straight back, with your chest over but not in front of the front knee. The same principle applies to the squat in the sense that when the front leg sinks and bends, the arch of the foot and the knee is actively pushed up and away from the body. When you return to the original position, push off your heel of the front leg. You can also step backwards with the same principle.

There are many variations on how to do the lunge; for instance you could stay in the position with an isometric contraction or do repetitions of sinking down and up again. The key is to be able to move functionally and safely so that lunging is beneficial and not a risk to injury. Weak buttocks and tight hip flexors will limit the stride of the lunge until being symmetrical is restored and movement patterns can be improved.

Summary

In this chapter I've shown the health benefits of exercise within our limits and how to progress those limits step by step, with the objective of becoming fitter and healthier. I've listed the normal entry levels and how to overcome challenges of niggling injuries or setbacks. This isn't an exhaustive list of exercises but a good guide to springboard you into action.

The main goal of this chapter is to break the conditioning that pain is inevitable as we age; pain is only inevitable if we become sedentary and lose our ability to move well as we age. This flawed limiting belief blindsides us into waiting until a problem arises before acting. Musculoskeletal pain is mostly caused by **prolonged sitting**, poor postural alignment, periods of inactivity over time and poor form when exercising. These can be singular problems or they can be combination problems interacting with each other.

Someone once told me an ounce of prevention is worth a pound of cure. By acting now, working towards being physically functional (joints and muscles moving well) and exercising regularly will reduce your risk of injury, will make you feel better mentally and will encourage and increase your chances of the best long-term health.

Physical education quiz

1) Exercise is described as?
a) Only beneficial when we already sick
b) Will reduce all-cause mortality
c) Make our lives shorter
d) Has no effect on our health

2) To unlock the benefits of regular exercise we need to?
a) Buy new running trainers and gym gear
b) Run a marathon
c) Be the strongest person in the gym
d) Walk for 30 minutes 4-5 times a week

3) Walking in nature will?
a) Cause a bad back
b) Cause us to develop asthma
c) Release chemicals that make us feel good
d) Release chemical that are bad for us

4) Prolonged sitting...?
a) Will extend your lifespan
b) Can be reversed by regular exercise
c) Is scientifically proven to be as bad as smoking cigarettes
d) Is scientifically proven to be good for lower back pain

5) When we are standing the centre of gravity line runs through?
a) The heart and forward of the belly button
b) The belly button and heart
c) The eyelashes
d) Only your GP knows

6) The cause of people's musculoskeletal neck or back pain is?
a) Their pillow
b) Their mattress
c) Not taking pain medication as a preventive measure
d) Their compensatory posture caused by misalignments of the spine

7) A foam roller is?
a) To build muscle
b) For cardiovascular fitness
c) Trigger point therapy
d) Only for athletes

8) The goal of remedial exercise is?
a) To advance toward functional fitness
b) To wait for an injury and then start

9) The saying goes 'an ounce of prevention...'?
a) Is a pound of cure
b) Is a pound of medication
c) Is an apple a day
d) Is the motto of the current healthcare system

10) Musculoskeletal pain is?
a) Is an absolute as we age
b) Is mostly caused by misalignments of our joints
c) Cannot be resolved and is for life
d) Is only resolved by cortical steroid injections

Psychology

I was with some friends once and a man appeared with two German shepherds. They were so inviting of our attention, everyone in the group had a moment acknowledging and admiring these sweet-natured dogs. I wondered out loud if all German shepherds were of a similar nature compared with other breeds and one friend said that with a considered approach, it is true if you show them kindness in their training. He then explained how dogs are a reflection of their training. It seems an obvious conclusion to make, but this had a profound effect on me, as I began to consider whether this is the same for humans.

This revived a long-held belief inside me that the nature of all humans is deep down to be thoughtful and kind, just as my friend believed all dogs to be. Our thoughts, emotions and behaviour are only a reflection of our own development and environment. When we miss our developmental stages, we act within the limitations of these missing pieces. What if I was to say that at any time in our life, it's not only possible to become aware of these missing pieces, but we can also acquire them, on a path to becoming a well-adjusted adult – how many would believe me?

This begs the question, what is a well-adjusted adult? In my mind this is an adult able to form healthy relationships, having the ability to be independent, to be socially aware and the ability to constructively reflect on their own behaviour. These are all learned behavioural skills that I believe people are capable of achieving with time, effort and honesty with themselves.

I believe with the correct support we are capable of consciously choosing our behaviour by becoming more aware of our thoughts, feelings and emotions. I also believe it's not about training ourselves to think or be a certain way; it is about the sage advice of **knowing thyself** and acting in accordance with who we are in our roots.

Understanding our own motives behind our actions will separate us from them, to see them merely for what they are, thoughts reacting to external stimuli real or not, and which only exist (perceived, interpreted and internalized) inside our own head. Below these fears and limiting beliefs is who we really are, deep within our self. This part of us is not bound by the human form and is pure peace and love. The more we can connect with this part of ourselves, the more we will outwardly act congruently with who we are meant to be.

I am experienced in this area, as I myself admit on occasion to suffering from a loss of mental wellness. I've included my own story here to give an example of a lineage of mental health and then afterwards I will explain the tools and understanding (non-pharmaceutical interventions) that helped me regain my mental wellness.

My story

Boyhood

When I was a child I suffered with shyness. I would find opening up to people or other kids I didn't know difficult. I subconsciously overcame this difficulty by developing a behavioural issue, namely hyperactivity. By being active I was able to overcome my self-consciousness, by being immersed in play. In this state of hyperactivity, I didn't know my boundaries and this increased the likelihood I would be in trouble.

I was the kid version of Dr Jekyll and Mr Hyde: an upstanding gentleman in Victorian London develops a potion, changing his personality into Mr Hyde, a person capable of committing crimes with no remorse. When the potion wears off Dr Jekyll regains consciousness and subsequently feels shame for the actions of Mr Hyde. When I was hyperactive, I was Mr Hyde Jnr, naughty for anyone supervising me, whereas when I was calm I was the Dr Jekyll Jnr, thoughtful and reflective.

Junior was also a bed-wetter to an age later than normal, as subconsciously he was scared of the dark. He feared leaving his bed because in his dreams, a hand would come out of the shadows and snatch him. He wasn't the only one, as one in ten children with a behavioural issue also has a bed-wetting issue. He didn't feel shame for this behaviour as a child but years later he would internalize this behaviour to be shameful, seeing himself through filters of being defective (filters explained page XXX).

Looking back I suspect Junior had a cerebellum (the word for 'little brain' in Latin) dysfunction, which is an underdevelopment of neurological wiring in that part of the brain, something which is more common in young children than we realize. This explained his slowness to grasp reading, a habit of poor spelling, poor concentration levels, messy handwriting, unruly behaviour, bed-wetting and shyness. I might add these were all things that he managed to overcome in time.

The cerebellum is the movement manager of the brain, coordinating balance and movement, and does this a million times faster than the cerebrum, which is used for thinking tasks like reading and writing and listening. When the cerebellum is underdeveloped the cerebrum (the thinking brain) has to cover for the cerebellum and instead of working on tasks like reading writing and listening, the cerebrum will prioritize processing movement over them. Hence children with cerebellum underdevelopment are slow at comprehension tasks and appear uncoordinated because their brain is working on a movement or balance task that is meant to be controlled by the cerebellum. When the cerebellum is controlling movement patterns the cerebrum can focus on developing and processing reading, writing and listening skills. The key is to improve cerebellum motor skill before expectations of reading, writing and listening well.

Education is still lagging behind on these understandings of cerebellum dysfunction, as seen when a child is identified with learning difficulties – they are often given earpieces and other aids which address the symptoms of the dysfunction but not the cause. If practitioners were to focus on advising specific movement exercises to develop the cerebellum, comprehension skills would come more easily to them regardless of the aids available.

As time went on, Junior became a teenager and naturally he became rebellious. Mr Hyde Jnr became a thief, as he began stealing money from his mum's purse. His mum's parents left her money as an inheritance, which she kept locked in her wardrobe, and he stole small amounts. There was a thrill in stealing, knowing he was doing wrong. Dr Jekyll Jnr would rationalize this money was pocket money of sorts and no one would ever know or that he would confess it in a book!

Those small amounts became a large sum of his mum's inheritance, enough that one day she was going to discover the truth. In the beginning Dr Jekyll Jnr was naïve to think that he could take this money and she wouldn't notice, but now that it was only a matter of time until his shameful behaviour was exposed, he worried what would happen when his nasty little habit was found out.

He felt guilty knowing that this money was from his mum's dead parents, given to her and not to him to spend. He wanted to stop, He would say to himself 'I'm not taking any more money' or 'I'm going to own up' but he never did. He continued to take money and eventually his mum did find out and she was upset because the money represented more the monetary value.

(Note: Discussing this with my mum years later the money wasn't an inheritance but I perceived at the time this to be the case.)

Junior was unable to separate events within his control and beyond him. He started to believe others' situations were his fault, running fantasies in his head that if he had done this or that, and been a better-behaved child (less like Mr Hyde Jnr) or made better decisions (stopped stealing), none of this would have happened. If he had discussed this with someone at the time, a resolution could have been reached, but he bottled his feelings and soldiered on.

Adulthood

I joined the Marines soon after leaving school and found bottling up my feelings a useful skill. In training I was encouraged to push myself further than I believed possible. It became like a drug, performing endurance and fatiguing tasks. This is how I learnt that exercise has a profound effect on our mood and feelings.

There was a culture in the Marines of work hard, play hard. We were taught to maintain focus, use our common sense, and look out for one another because one day these skills might save our lives. As mentioned in chapter one (the philosophy chapter) this is the premise of the 'can-do' attitude in the military mindset. We drilled routinely so that if the time ever came in battle we would be brave enough to function effectively and be prepared to improvize as the situation dictated.

In our downtime each troop would go to the pub once a week for a social gathering. We got to know each other better and the pub was a social leveller because all ranks spoke amongst one another without feeling superior. We were a family of sorts, working and socializing together.

I feel blessed for these experiences; I had many friends and learnt a lot about life, but leaving was a significant junction on my path. I had to leave to grow personally and professionally. These years taught me the value of order, fitness and friendship. The next stage of my life would be to take these lessons and develop them into the philosophy that is Stoical Beingism. That road would be long and the first step would be transitioning to civilian life, but first I had to heal some old wounds.

Life was difficult in the beginning after the Marines, learning the structure and rules of civilian life. I understand first hand why so many ex-service personal struggle when they leave the military. Although we develop discipline, common sense and teamwork, many of us are still underdeveloped emotionally, sometimes because of our background.

The military provides a surrogate parental stability while people are serving. When they leave and this structure isn't there, they struggle because they lack emotional stability and quite often use coping mechanisms to manage this lack. In civilian life the routine and drill of the military, which gave their life meaning, is absent, and suddenly this meaning disappears. This is what people commonly call being institutionalized: when someone struggles to live and function normally outside of this network.

I was without vocational qualifications, and lacking the stability of the military, I felt like I was walking off a cliff edge in the mist. I also began to feel a resentment towards life, but I wasn't sure of the origin of those feelings. Over the years I had put my unresolved feelings into a blind spot and now they were coming into view and were more difficult to control. I couldn't pinpoint what and where the origin of these thoughts and emotions I was experiencing was, and I felt overwhelmed (communication page XXX).

I would be upset on reflection that I wasn't acting congruently with the person I thought I was. I would feel guilty and punish myself for my behaviour. I had internalized the shame from my childhood and never resolved those feelings and they were manifesting in an eternal struggle of reacting to circumstances and punishing myself for those reactions.

The future seemed uncertain in this new world. I had a tendency to become paranoid and self-destructive, burning bridges with people only trying to help me, with stories in my head that everyone was against me or wanted me to fail. I would twist events that had no foundation or evidence to fit into a 'why me?' attitude (philosophy page XXX).

I identified with these thoughts and could not separate myself from them (distancing page XXX) and therefore could not challenge them (challenging page XXX). In desperation I was reaching for coping mechanisms, drinking alcohol not for the reason I used to with my friends in the Marines. I was too scared to process my unresolved hurt and pain of the past (sensations page XXX). Eventually there was an acceptance. I reached a point of surrender.

There was a moment where I gave up fighting. I conceded to accepting there was a problem and I felt like the world's biggest loser. However, once this passed something changed, and a weight was lifted from my shoulders. The fight within me was over and I felt a relief. I had internalized a limiting belief that if I admitted weakness people would know my secret shame. Once I became aware of my resistance to admitting a problem, I reacted less to this internalized belief that was causing unwanted behaviours. I was able to step outside of myself and begin to view things objectively, therefore distancing myself.

I began working with a psychotherapist to help me process my unresolved resentment and separate myself from what I could control and what was beyond my control, although at the time I could not describe this in these terms. I realized the feelings of shame I was feeling as a child or as an adult were only a reaction to how I felt about myself and they did not represent me. They were caused by a limiting self-belief that I was not worthy or good enough, which I was covering up with bravado. I was introduced to dream interpretation, which I thought was powerful messages from our subconscious, attempting to make sense of the world.

I started to journal regularly, mostly about the resentment I felt. My writing was angry, full of grief, but one day I felt different and my journaling turned from anger to understanding and then forgiveness. I had manifested my anger through writing and once I had processed this, through communicating with myself through journaling, my anger faded and in its place I felt forgiveness and a renewed love for life.

As a chiropractic student I was treated regularly on my course and it was clear to me this also helped heal my emotional wounds. I had spiritual experiences after treatment, where I felt lighter, high almost, shifting how I felt. The choices I was making since leaving the Marines were opening me up in ways I hadn't considered before. Along with my journaling and working with a psychotherapist, I was growing as a person. I realized it was never about destroying or crushing another part of me, it was about acknowledging and integrating parts of me that felt shameful and unworthy.

I realized from a young age I had constructed walls to protect a sensitive part of myself to manage the symptom of shyness, caused by a deep-seated fear of shame, that I was defective and unworthy. I removed those walls piece by piece, but I also realized those walls were constructed by an old part of myself at a young age, acting in my best interest, and I acknowledged them with gratitude. I asked for their forgiveness and renewed my bond with them.

I look back on this part of my adulthood as one of great turmoil, drama and darkness. If I could relive those times, I would act differently, using the emotional skills I've developed to resolve the resentment I felt, instead of spilling them out uncontrollably and as a consequence hurting others. I had to go through this to learn those lessons and be who I am now. In the Marines I wore a uniform and there was structure, but at the beginning of civilian life, I had to find my own uniform and structure.

Coming full circle

I was lost on my path but when I found myself again I was much clearer about who I was and I had a renewed commitment to the direction I wanted to take my life. I had learnt an ability to process emotions in the moment instead of bottling them and letting them build up to eventual emotional triggers. I learnt I was not processing my emotions and instead I was avoiding them by putting them in a blind spot.

I was functioning but if I wanted to grow as a person I needed to address this habit of avoidance. By learning about my own psychology I was able to separate my own feelings from other people's, instead of taking them on as my own – and in doing so I could help other people more.

In some ways I am only describing the process of growing up, a rite of passage to understanding myself and stepping into my manhood. These insights were not instant, as they came over many years, only when I was ready to see them. I monitored and reflected on my internal dialogue for my reactions and negative attitudes, tracing them back to understand their cause without judging myself.

My path to awareness doesn't mean I never feel triggered by situations. I am limited to a human form, flesh and bone, thoughts and feelings, therefore susceptible to irrational and rational fears. When I do experience difficult situations, I am aware of my emotions and can reflect on them, I am able to distance and communicate with myself and others what I am feeling, and I am able to challenge my thoughts and feelings (processing emotion) at the time or on reflection.

Despite some people's air of impenetrability, I guarantee even those people from time to time suffer with insecurities, irrational fear, self-doubt and negative attitudes. An ideal upbringing only means a person is less susceptible to developing unhealthy patterns of behaviour than those less fortunate. If people hit their developmental markers and heal their childhood resentments, they will generally be better at managing their emotions, than someone who is carrying around unresolved emotional issues and in some cases is only aware of the behaviour and not the cause.

An ideal childhood in my opinion is a balance of nurturing and challenges. A child insulated from challenges and the child overwhelmed by them are both children that will potentially miss their developmental markers because they are missing the mental and emotional skills that healthy nurture and challenges bring.

Antidepressants

With this awareness of mental health I understand myself better, and I understand others better. I don't mean this egoistically but I figured this out by initiating my own interventions for educating myself, journaling and using a therapist. I had to because of the lack of mental health awareness and inadequate interventions by the traditional medical model.

When I had this insight I realized why so many people are on antidepressant medication; they admit to an awareness of a mental health problem, which is a step towards healing, but when they visit a GP, in many cases they are labelled for life with a mental health disorder and they are prescribed medication in the first instance.

This was my experience when I approached a GP with my insight and I was sent away with a prescription for antidepressants. The healthcare system made little effort to help me understand my own situation and feelings, or to discover alternatives to antidepressant medication, which for many becomes a lifelong accepted label and solution.

I was determined to overcome my mental health issues with the same determination that I approached recruit training, and to make whatever label of mental health I was experiencing at the time into a fluid label instead of being a victim to mental health label.

A few years later I read a *Times* article regarding mental health and learnt many reporters were taking routine antidepressant medication for anxiety and depression, but also stronger and more addictive drugs like diazepam and lithium on a daily basis to manage their mood, as a lifelong solution – meaning they had no end date to stop taking this medication.

I respect the reporter's openness but the article read almost like they wore their prescriptions as a badge of honour. This chapter is about learning about the cause of mental health issues and building a strategy to managing our emotional state as an alternative to pharmaceutical solutions. There is an alternative to antidepressants and I am living proof of this.

Psychological self-help manual

When I talk about feeling triggered what I mean is our internal protection mode is turned on, called fight or flight, which is explained at the beginning of Biology (chapter 3 page XXX). Protection mode is triggered by our fears regardless of whether they are rational or irrational. To survive and navigate through life, feeling fear is a natural reaction to stressful situations. These fears come from our innate need to survive and if our survival is in doubt, real or not, we will be compelled to go into protection mode.

Feeling triggered in reaction to a situation might include a difficulty to think straight, panicking in the moment and acting rashly, due to feeling fear, worry or anxiety – this is normal. When we feel unsettled in such circumstances we may interpret the situation differently than normal, causing us to act out of character, hurting ourselves or those close to us, which we wouldn't otherwise do.

Survival response	Peaceful response
Awareness:	
Fear of injury (psychological or physical) or total loss of life	Total being content
Chemical:	
Chain reaction for stress hormones in preparations of fight or flight	Relaxation response

*awareness and chemical response explained page XXX

Everyone experiences triggers

People do not need a personality disorder to feel triggered emotionally. When we are scared by a loud noise this is an example of the beginnings of a triggered psychological and a physical, chemical response, by causing you in a split second to hold your breath or take a sharp inhale and for your heart to skip a beat. Once the threat has been determined to be real or not, within seconds we can psychologically control the physical response and avoid going into fight or flight. We often laugh about the irrational thought of being scared by the loud noise.

Someone could be perfectly stable emotionally and then because of life events their mental wellbeing declines, potentially impacting primary relationships and friendships. If a loved one died we would understandably mourn; grieving is a natural process to go through and suppressing grief can do more harm than good.

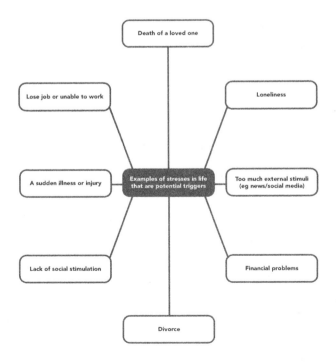

We will all experience triggers throughout a lifetime as human beings; grief is one example, but others include feeling unloved, fearing for our safety or fear of being abandoned. These are just some examples of how triggers can manifest themselves. How life normally works is that we go through periods of relative normality and then every so often we experience episodes of unpredictable emotional situations, which we react to.

It's not about never feeling triggered in the future, it's about learning how to be a human being by understanding if our survival is in doubt; real or not, we are going to feel fear in accordance with that doubt. Through accepting this when these fears arise we can process them even if at the time we feel overwhelmed by them.

With this knowledge when intense emotions manifest, we can understand their origin, and we can distance ourselves without avoiding them by acknowledging and challenging them. If we upset others in our triggered state, we can communicate our behaviour afterwards, limiting the damage caused to those relationships.

Observing thoughts

In the ancient Eastern cultures we are considered not to be just our thoughts or our feelings; we are someone much deeper. We are the observer of those thoughts and feelings and this observer is not bound by the human form; therefore they transcend the fear of survival. The mind is a chatterbox when observed, constantly attempting to make sense of situations, ideas and feelings. When we are calm, we will feel balanced with our internal dialogue but when we are triggered this voice is prone to becoming irrational and unpredictable and will sway us to act out of character, in an attempt to protect us from this perceived threat to survival.

Just like when a migraine sufferer can feel the warning signs of a migraine, they usually go to a dark room and lie down until the migraine has pasted. The same is with an emotionally charged situation. I advise stopping what you are doing and where appropriate remove you from the situation because there is a tipping point before the emotional trigger. Just like a migraine sufferer can spot the signs and prevent or lessen the effects of a migraine, the same is with a highly emotionally charged situation, as this can be minimized by acting early in response to the signs.

I know from my own experience that if I remove myself from the stimuli I can lessen the effects and I can begin the process of separating myself from the situation, before taking any further actions or decisions. When we are calm it's easier to distinguish between our thoughts that are relevant and thoughts that are reactive.

Being able to reflect on our behaviour is the key to filling these gaps that on occasions are in our blind spot, which means we may not even be aware of our behaviour. In my case I could only resolve the resentment in my blind spot once I was ready to face it. Thoughts and emotions enter a blind spot because there is no method available to the person to resolve them with their current emotional intelligence.

The blind spot exists for these thoughts that trigger a threat to survival. For this reason drawing people out of the blind spot makes them feel anxious (triggering survival mode) so most just leave them where they are and unconsciously accept the behaviour they cause.

Creating a safe environment to share thoughts, feelings and emotions is the first step to uncovering our own blind spots and the limiting beliefs behind them. Reflecting on past stressful situations, describing your thoughts and feelings you experienced at the time without fear of being judged, will help you heal and understand yourself. With practice you'll develop insight into those experiences and as time goes on you will be able to reflect in real time, so that you can make better choices.

With practice and understanding, being able to spot the warning signs (psychological changes) in advance will reduce the potential arousal of the fight or flight (physical changes) response in real time.

Filters

There is no reality other than what we perceive to be real. Let me explain. Two people in identical situations are given a compliment; the first person receives this with a filter of 'rose-tinted glasses', making them feel good about themselves. The second person receives the compliment with a filter of 'not being good enough', which focus on the mistakes they made or how they could have done better. They reject the compliment to fit with a filter that they are somehow not good enough to receive a compliment.

Filters consciously and subconsciously control how we perceive the world and determine how we feel and the choices we make. Even the thoughts you are thinking at the moment are being filtered; this is how we make sense of the world. As in the example above, some filters are more helpful than others.

Filters are beliefs we hold about ourselves and the world, which aren't necessarily true but we internalize them to be true. They are often without any rational proof or supporting evidence. When we are unaware of them, we accept them without question as an absolute truth, even if this truth is seen as different in reality to others. Filters are potential emotional triggers to a fear of a threat to survival, which others might perceive as unnecessarily overreacting, because they do not see the fear or limiting belief.

In emotional and stressful situations people draw conclusions that they would otherwise not; they are more prone to make a rash decision, and therefore regret their actions and be hypercritical of themselves afterwards, and will project this filter onto others. They fight and react instead of being in surrender to the thoughts and actions of filters.

Filters only exist in our heads and can be difficult to describe, or in my case I was too ashamed to discuss them when I was younger. When they are communicated, recalling sensations of anger, grief and pride to name a few can be internally volatile and scary, and we might feel triggered recalling them, but only by describing them can we value them. Living with a distorted view of reality often leaves a person feeling isolated and alone, when what they want to communicate is the opposite of this.

Similar to the stress and relaxation response, filters can be positive and negative. Learning about them will help us understand our behaviour without biased judgment of those filters, helping us be more in control of our life. Overleaf is a list of opposite filters:

Filters

Negative	Positive
Belief of being unloved	Feeling loved
Fearing for safety	Feeling safe
Paranoia (people are conspiring against them)	Feeling supported
Not being good enough	Feeling worthy
Being a dependant/need others to make decisions for you	Confident in decisions
Self sacrificing excessively	Valuing self
Only perfectionism will do/focus on negatives	Being tolerant
Sense of entitlement	Feeling humble

Distancing

Distancing is a process of separating from our fearful emotions to minimize our psychological and physiological reaction to a situation. By distancing we step out of the role of a fearful actor or actress and we can take control of the script and direct, instead of being directed by our survival filters. Distancing means reflecting on our behaviour without judgment, to resolve these thoughts without fighting them. When we resist the emotion we are reacting to them, which makes those thoughts stick to us and the more we repel or avoid them, the more likely they are to cause an emotional trigger.

Think of this like we are all living in our own movie of mental health, and having good mental health is to be in control of the script, director, role and scenes. When we lose control of these roles we are forced to act them out uncomfortable situations in a film called 'Being Human'. The world becomes distorted to fit the storyline surrounding us because we are unable to separate from our human state. As I wrote earlier, in Eastern philosophy we are not our thoughts, we are someone deeper than our human form.

Storylines in this movie include we are not good enough, we are not loved or we fear being abandoned: these are just a few examples of situations our human may find themselves in. Sometimes our human never leaves the film set, acting out a character that isn't really them, but because they are consistently this character people know them as this, further reinforcing behaviours and perceptions that are not necessarily them.

Being aware of your thoughts but not identifying with them is a powerful tool, by observation of thought we are able maintain our emotional balance more often. When I spot myself experiencing negative thoughts, I distance myself from them and realize they do not represent me, I recognizing they are filters manifesting themselves, they do not need fighting or eradicating, they only need to be acknowledged and channeled into my greater good. At this point I normally naturally find myself taking a deep breath, this coincides with stepping out of the character fearing for survival, which does not represent me, but I accept is a part of me wanting to protect me.

When we feel triggered by intense emotional situations we might feel like we're in a horror film or a thriller, in the sense that we unable to escape the fear we are feeling, causing us to freeze or act irrationally and rashly. A common coping mechanism is to give in to fear, in an attempt to regain our safety. The threat which is perceived, real or not, is overwhelming, therefore changing our behaviour, and this is an example of how and when events enter our blind spot. The overwhelming fear cannot be processed without triggering us so we subconsciously use avoidance behaviour.

Distancing is not avoiding. When we avoid our thoughts, feeling and emotions they go into a blind spot, which is a place for unresolved thoughts when a person is without the skills to resolve them. On the other hand, distancing means recognizing our thoughts but not identifying with them so that those thoughts do not overwhelm us.

Communication

As noted earlier, in my own story I used journaling and a psychotherapist to communicate what I was feeling. Being able to communicate thoughts, feeling and emotions will help you balance your mental wellness. Here I will give examples of emotions we feel and describe them in a journal format so that you can do the same. By journaling these emotional markers over time they will become a framework of recognizing and limiting our triggers to stimuli.

Journaling is so powerful: by writing down the feelings from about thoughts you are distancing, in doing so you are able to act as your own therapist. When I suggest journaling to people they normally don't because they fear others will know their confidential thoughts and risk being betrayed or they don't know how or where to start. I say start by writing what you're feeling – you can still benefit from journaling without writing down confidential information because you can write about how these confidential thoughts make you feel. Here are some examples:

When I am journaling I know the difference between shame and grief because when I feel shame, I feel anxious, I become skittish and I lose my attention span. However, when I feel grief I feel depressed instead of anxious, I lose my motivation and energy for tasks that I normally care about – they become of no interest to me as I lose my long-term focus.

When I feel anger I feel a whoosh rise up through my chest that extends into my head. I guess that makes sense because when people depict a person being angry they sometimes draw them with a red face and steam exploding from their ears. It's normally a moment of short duration and sometimes I'm surprised at the trivial nature of my anger.

When I feel fear there is a sinking feeling in my stomach, I feel my pulse rise and my heart beat in my chest is noticeable. My awareness becomes vigilant to any threats in the environment and how to restore my safety. When the feeling of fear has passed I usually feel exhausted and tired, which is my body attempting to reset, rest and digest.

When I feel guilt I punish myself unnecessarily by being unreasonably hard on myself using 'parental regret': 'I should have done this' or 'I should have done that'. I leave no room to learn from my mistakes, as my punishment is to believe myself not worthy of learning, as some twisted justice needs to be restored. I lack forgiveness, understanding and tolerance.

One of my favourite emotions is hope. It's such an uplifting feeling and it's easy to feel joyful about the present and the future. There is a flow and rhythm to hope that makes me feel strong physically and emotionally. There's an acceptance that what will be will be, but a hope that it will work out for me and others. I'm motivated, I'm focused and I'm a joy to be around. If I could bottle hope then I would.

When I feel thankful toward others I feel humbled and a connectedness with the source of my gratitude. I feel the opposite to fear by feeling lightness in my stomach and I feel uplifted; this is usually accompanied by an insight. When I receive gratitude from others I feel humble and a renewed life purpose. When I am calm I feel balanced and I feel clarity about who I am and the direction of my path. With clarity I also feel compassion and empathy for others and will want to help where possible.

Here is an extract from a journal I wrote to give you an example how this might help you:

When I feel thoughts, feelings and emotions that do not serve me, I recognize them and I honour them for their service. They are usually a survival mindset, fear based, to protect me from harm. They perceive danger, a threat to my survival. They act in my best interests. I give this part of myself love and when I do I rise above survival mode.

I forgive these perceptions that are not real and are only real in my imagination, which is using a slippery slope to the worst case scenario. If the perceptions are based on evidence, and are real, I forgive them too. In doing so I rise above the sorrow and resolve my fears, which will increase my capacity to give love into the world.

With this new insight, I am complete. I can better serve my goal by letting go of worries, fears that I am not enough. I can step into my power without fear of failing or that I am not loved.

Each time I recognize these perceptions, I will process them by letting them go with honour or encouraging them with love. By doing so I am integrating them into my life, cross-referencing them with my values, principles and my goal.

These perceptions real or not, are about me, which isn't in alignment with my goal. My goal is so much bigger than my own ego of thoughts, feelings and emotions.

You will notice here I do not reveal any confidential information about what has caused these fears and the insights that came through experiencing them. I am not suggesting avoiding revealing situations and circumstances, I am merely removing the barrier that people fear others will judge them if they read their journal. The power of journaling can be instant and on other occasions can take time. I suggest being consistent and to make time daily in a safe place to write. At this point people normally say 'What will I write about?' If you're experiencing triggers, start by describing how they make you feel and the ruminating and recurring thoughts that lead up to the trigger.

Emotions are the language of what we are feeling. Being able to describe an emotion will help us prevent triggers and let you and others understand what you are experiencing.

Sensations

Sensations are informative as to what emotions we are experiencing, which are in turn a result of our thoughts. By naming our feelings we can trace them back to the thought or filter that is causing them. Certain thoughts that do not serve us manifest the same feeling every time. By identifying the feeling attached to the emotion and thought pattern, we are able to practise distancing, instead of reaching the tipping point of feeling triggered and making ourselves potentially unwell.

Challenging

Challenging is an extension of distancing by not only acknowledging our thoughts but judging if those thoughts serve us or not. When we distance from our thoughts we can question whether what we are feeling is supported by evidence or just an assumption. When we are triggered or stuck in a filter our thoughts more often than not will be misleading, irrational and not supported by evidence. Reality will be distorted to make a situation mean something different from when we are calm and balanced emotionally. In this highly charged emotional state a person will believe a thought to be true and especially unable to believe that this thought is not true.

Examples of Sensations as Markers of Emotion state

Butterflies
Lump in throat
Feeling a chill
Feeling faint or weakness
Tingling
Heat or sweating
Nausea
Skin crawling
Disorientated

Examples of Sensations as Markers of Symptoms

Indigestion
Upset stomach
Bloating
Heartburn
Grinding teeth
Over eating, under eating
Headache
Dizziness
Blurred vision
Tinnitus
Shortness of breath
Changes in normal heart rate, fast or slow

Challenging our thoughts in real time or on reflection will question our behaviour constructively so that we can make a better choice next time.

Questioning objectively, is this an absolute truth or only real in my head?

→ How many people would agree this is to be the case?
→ Imagine if 100 people on the TV game show *Family Fortunes*'s survey were asked is this true: how many would agree?
→ What would a jury think?
→ Would a person I admire believe this about themselves?
→ Is this something I've experienced before?
→ Do I recognize this as filter?

Writing down how and what we were feeling at the time of the trigger can offer further insight and also speaking with someone we trust is another useful way to challenge our thoughts.

In my experience I wouldn't practise challenging thoughts: first learn about awareness, filters and distancing so as to build a framework of your thoughts and feelings personal to you. Everybody is different and only you experience your thoughts, feelings and emotions; people can help you, but they can only help you if you 'know thyself'.

My 10 psychology recommendations

1. Reflect on your own past non-judgmentally to assess possible triggers of current thoughts feelings and behaviours.
2. Focus on the underlying cause of the behaviour by talking events through with a trusted confidant.
3. Learn about filters, distancing, communications, bodily sensations and challenging techniques when managing your own thoughts, feelings and emotions.
4. Practise a stoic mindset by acknowledging your thoughts, feeling and emotions and know that when triggered these will pass. Commit to a determination to work through this situation.

5. When triggered (survival response) remove yourself from the situation or circumstances to regroup and switch back to rest and digest, and only then re-engage.

6. Take a lead in your own mental health by learning about psychology (see first three recommendations) and don't just rely on the advice of a specialist or on antidepressants.

7. Avoid landing on labels and only use a marker of where you are currently at to describe your occurring behavior.

8. Act before crisis point; if in the past there has been a history of feelings triggering the survival response, or anxiety and depression, seek help now by learning and using a therapist.

9. The race is long and in the end it's only with you: focus on improving your own mental health journey by reducing stimuli such as social media and TV.

10. We are limited to a human form therefore everyone experiences pain and suffering from time to time. Be kind to yourself and acknowledge that the pain and suffering we feel is only a perception of how we view reality.

Techniques to manage emotions and mood

Breathing

The first thing to address in emotional situations is our breathing. When we are relaxed we will breathe into our lower lungs, which contractions the diaphragm. However, when we are stressed emotionally we will take shallower breaths that do not fully utilize the diaphragm and use other muscles in our neck and shoulders. This is why people who are stressed on regular basis feel tight muscles in their neck and shoulders.

When we are stressed our breathing quickens, we usually breathe through our mouths, and at cellular level we consume more oxygen. Breathing through our nose means we not only slow our breath, we also use less oxygen at cellular level, and more oxygen is diffused into our bloodstream via the lungs. The air we breathe through the nose is filtered more than when we breathe through our mouth because of the hairs in our nostrils. Also behind the nose is moisture and mucus glands that again filter the air we breathe.

Spend a few minutes in a relaxed environment breathing through the nose, inhaling to a count of 4-6 and exhaling for the same count; consciously this will slow your breathing and activate the diaphragm. Standing, lying down or sitting on your back, completely relax into the exercise and observing your thoughts and sensations. Focused breathing over minutes becomes longer and deeper and you will feel relaxation. When breathing, focus on raising the belly on inhaling and lowering it on the exhale, to a similar count.

Meditation (mindfulness)

Mindfulness as meditation is a secular adaptation from the teachings of meditation in Buddhism and Hinduism. These techniques are proven to outperform antidepressant medication, and be more cost effective without side effects. The premise of mindfulness is similar to distancing in that during meditation the user is observing thoughts but not reacting to them. The focus is on remaining in the present time and observing feelings as present moment sensations.

Mindfulness switches off the psychological fear of the survival response, which in turn switches off the chemical chain reaction of the fight or flight response (page XXX biology) and instead switches on the chemical chain reaction for the relaxation response. With regular mindfulness, our brain will build connections to control this switch so that we are less likely to experience emotional triggers.

I had a daily Vipassana practice for many years and found this very helpful in balancing my life and emotions. I always felt re-energized with clarity after meditation. Meditation is easier than people think and has many long-term benefits, such as slowing the progress of age-related cognitive diseases.

Make some time to relax (reduce digital stimuli)

Make some time to detach from life's stresses that does not involve screen time or computers. By all means if you find them relaxing then continue these, but it's also good be able to relax without. Simple pleasures like reading a book, making time to talk in nature with ourselves or with a loved one, playing cards with family or friends are a few examples of how previous generations took time out.

The reason I say this is because screen time can be like a diet of junk food – addictive and unhealthy – and when we get addicted to junk food, healthy food doesn't taste that good anymore. Too much screen time makes us not appreciate the simple, non-digital pleasures.

Regular exercise

We touched on the benefits of exercise in Physical Education, but it's worth mentioning again because they are not limited to physical benefits; exercise is also excellent for our mental and emotion wellbeing. Along with keeping us in good physical shape, which is proven to prevent many health issues, exercise makes us feel good; therefore we are less likely to feel overwhelmed by stress, anxiousness or depressed emotionally. People who exercise regularly are more likely to be alert, think clearly and feel confident in their decisions.

Even mild-to-moderate exercise such as walking for 30 minutes a day multiple times a week has been shown to unlock these benefits to our mental health. Exercise is as vital to your health as brushing your teeth. If you're feeling anxious moving is sometimes the best remedy.

Eating

In the modern world a common coping mechanism to psychological dis-ease is overeating to overcome our feelings of anxiousness and depression, leading to physical ill health issues. When this happens a person is more than likely eating highly stimulating and addictive foods, which are unnatural compared with a balanced diet. A diet of fresh vegetables, protein, oats and fibre is an excellent option for improving mood and physical health. Sometime eating is useful when experiencing an emotional trigger to settle and ground us.

Sleep

Resting is as vital as exercising and eating healthily and all three affect one another. When we are exercising regularly with a balanced diet, sleep will come naturally to us. This is because you are more than likely in control of your stress levels and emotions. When we are not in control of our emotional chemistry in the short term, we are more likely to feel adrenaline spikes that make sleeping difficult. In the long term someone sleep deprived is more likely to be obese and have an increased likelihood of illnesses such as diabetes, heart disease and dementia.

Remember dis-ease comes before disease (page XXX prospectus). If we are stuck in fight or flight the body neglects the house cleaning and essential maintenance needed. The first four hours of sleep are so the body can rest and repair and the brain uses this time to flush out toxins. Studies show that animals will die of sleep deprivation before starvation.

Routine is a useful tool to improving the quality of night-time sleeping. Encourage calmness before bedtime, by avoiding technology an hour beforehand. If there are stimuli for potential triggers such as emails or text, avoid them before bed. Make time for those tasks and ground yourself beforehand with a breathing technique.

Summary

I've shared details about myself to give a real-life case study for the benefits of learning, not only about psychology but your personal psychology that is unique to you. We can describe what we are feeling to others but only you feel the experience of what you are experiencing. I hope my story inspires you to become more understanding of your fears.

Putting these tools together is a way we can not only manage our emotional state but also to reflect and learn to overcome them and make better choices in the future. Normally feelings of anxiety and depression are reactions to our thoughts; by acknowledging and distancing from those thoughts and feelings we are able to communicate (interpret them) and challenge them over their validity.

Combining these tools takes time and many learning cycles. Just by being aware of them is raising our consciousness.

Psychology quiz

1) A well-adjusted adult...?
a) Is dependent on others
b) Is bitter towards others
c) Has a habit of destroying relationships
d) Has the ability to be independent

2) Antidepressants?
a) Address the cause of your feelings
b) Chemically control your feelings
c) Will give you insight into your reason for taking them
d) Are better than meditation and regular exercise for resolving depression

3) An emotional trigger is?
a) An overreaction to circumstances
b) No psychological and physiological change to stress
c) Something that only happens to people that admit to mental health issues
d) Psychological and physiological change to stress

4) A filter is?
a) A perceived belief about the world that isn't necessarily true
b) An absolute truth about you
c) Is your identity for life and cannot be changed
d) Is a lack of intelligence

5) Distancing is described as?
a) Social distancing
b) Physically distancing
c) Separating from internal thoughts
d) Staying two car lengths back when driving

6) Challenging is?
a) Questioning a statement or belief to its validity
b) Judging ourselves unfairly
c) Aggressively confronting yourself
d) Punishing ourselves

7) Communication is described as?
a) Avoiding our unresolved thoughts and emotions
b) Describing what we are feeling to ourselves and others
c) Feeling anxious about talking to others
d) Can only be achieved by mentally well people

8) Sensations are?
a) Markers of what others are feeling
b) To be avoided and unacknowledged
c) Markers of what we are feeling
d) Only something emotionally sensitive people experience

9) Meditation is described as?
a) Resetting back to rest and digest
b) Resetting to fight or flight
c) Focusing on anger
d) A means to manifest increasing our income

10) Sleep is described as?
a) Provides no function
b) Laziness
c) Meant to be stressful with broken sleep
d) The body resting and recuperating

CERTIFICATE
OF ACHIEVEMENT

By reading this book in its
entirety you are awarded

Commonsense of
Essentials of Health
From The Inside Out

Awarded by The Back Doctor
Principal

David Tennison

Closing address

Thank you for your attendance on my health course. I hope you enjoyed this read as much as I did writing this book. Before we move onto the conclusion of this course and the awards ceremony, we started with a quote from Charlie Chaplin and I would like to finish with more wise words from the great man:

'At this juncture, I think it appropriate to sum up the state of the world as I see it today. The accumulating complexities of modern life, the kinetic invasion of the twentieth century finds the individual hemmed in by gigantic institutions that threaten from all sides, politically, scientifically and economically. We are becoming the victims of soul-conditioning of sanctions and permits.

This matrix into which we have allowed ourselves to be cast is due to a lack of cultural insight. We have gone blindly into ugliness and congestion and have lost our appreciation of the aesthetic. Our living sense has been blunted by profit, power and monopoly. We have permitted these forces to envelop us with an utter disregard of the ominous consequences.

Science, without thoughtful direction or sense of responsibility, has delivered up to politicians and the *militaire* weapons of such destruction that they hold in their hands the destiny of every living thing on this earth.

This plethora of power is given into the hands of *men* whose moral responsibility and intellectual competence are to say the least not infallible, and in many cases questionable, could end in a war of extermination of all life on earth. Yet we go blindly on.

As Dr Robert Oppenheimer once told me: "*Man* is driven by a compulsion to know". Well and good – but in many cases with a disregard for the consequences. With this the Doctor agreed. Some scientists are like religious fanatics. They rush ahead, believing that what they will discover is always for good and that their credo to know is a moral one.

Man is an animal with primary instincts of survival. Consequently, his ingenuity has developed first and his soul afterwards. Thus the progress of science is far ahead of man's ethical behavior.

Altruism is slow along the path of human progress. It ambles and stumbles along after science. And only by force of circumstances is it allowed to function. Poverty was not reduced by altruism or philanthropy of governments, but by the forces of dialectic materialism.

Carlyle said that the salvation of the world will be brought about by people thinking. But in order to bring this about, *man* must be forced into serious circumstances.

Thus *in* splitting the atom, *he* is driven into a corner and made to think. *He has* the choice to destroy *himself* or to behave *himself*; momentum of science is forcing *him* to make this decision. And under these circumstances, I believe that eventually *his* altruism will survive and *his* good-will towards mankind will triumph.'

This extract is taken from the book Charles Chaplin, My Autobiography, *in chapter thirty. These words were written in the sixties during the cold war but they read as if they were written yesterday. Thank you, Charlie.* My Autobiography *Copyright © Bubbles Incorporated S.A. Reproduced with permission.*

Conclusion

100 years from now

It's impossible to predict the future; all that can be said is times change and so do the truths we agree on. Judging by history, what is true today will be replaced with a new truth tomorrow, relevant for the times of future generations. I've outlined in this book the essential elements that I believe are missing from our educational system that in future I would like everyone to know, based on their significance to our health. Improving everyone's knowledge is how we can weed out unsound truths for better ones.

The medical system in its current form is antiquated and outdated, in my opinion. To wait for people to become sick, to not educate in health as a subject to people from a young age, to be performing questionable and unnecessary treatments and surgeries as short-term fixes, all means healthcare is not working in our long-term best interests.

This short-sightedness is influenced by the power and influence of the pharmaceutical industry. I live in hope that we the public can break free of this stranglehold and I believe the solution is increasing our own knowledge of health through education.

The dominance big business has over our education system is limiting our community spirit, bypassing democracy by influencing policy and stifling innovation for an evolving greater good. Big business is only interested in its own version of the greater good, which is centred on its own power in the market, and on profit margin.

Enough profit will never be enough for these companies, until they swallow up all competition at any cost to their own gain, regardless of the cost to our communities and our environment. They pretend with popular pledges and soundbites on whatever fad is hot at the moment to tug our heartstrings so that we can spend more money with them. I implore you to see through this illusion.

If the UK government is not going to encourage change in our education and healthcare system then we the public must take the initiative by learning about our health to protect our loved ones and culture. There is a saying 'each one, teach one', which was a saying in the 19th century within the black slave community. If a person was taught how to read they would pass their learning on by teaching someone else to read. I'm asking you to do the same, if there is a teaching from this book that resonates with you then please pass this information onto another.

The here and now

What's in this book isn't rocket science. I've presented simple truths that if more people knew or believed in, people would be healthier and happier and they would live longer. If we can improve everyone's base level of understanding, the more likely individual power can trump faceless organizations and their thought control.

A percentage of our income, our taxes, is being wasted on fruitless, short-term fixes that benefit the few and not the many because government supports big business, and as a consequence we the public are not receiving the best long-term return on our contribution. Imagine I gave someone a grocery list with money to pay for those items and they came back with sweets and cigarettes and then tried to convince me that's what I needed instead.

In my opinion the government is doing that with our taxes; £133 billion to be exact and still healthcare is being run down and failing. By improving our knowledge we can give the government a list of what we want for our taxes in a healthcare system and stop the abuse by big business that would have Clement Attlee turning in his grave.

A new healthcare order

It's logical to me that a patient-centred, proactive (cause-focused) system would be an upgrade on the current healthcare model. In a proactive system we could mine data to prevent many diseases and mould healthcare to develop better treatment plans, before problems start, monitoring the pre-emptive signs and symptoms which are precursors to disease.

As outlined in the introduction to the Hybrid Practitioner (chapter 4), I use kinesiology testing to make the most precise corrections for each person and this has served me well. Kinesiology is highly accurate, as accurate as any randomized controlled trial (RCT) for pharmaceuticals. Kinesiology could be used in a wider setting to fast track answers for developing a new healthcare system.

To show the power of kinesiology there is a repeatable test where artificial sweetener is placed in front or near someone (they and the tester do not know the contents via a third person) in an envelope; the tested muscles will go weak during a kinesiology test. However, if artificial sweetener is exchanged for vitamin C, the muscles will go strong on testing.

Somehow without consciously knowing, the subconscious part of us is able to bypass our conscious thoughts and filters, to determine the difference between a substance that is harmful or good for us. We still do not know how this happens, but from my own experience I've come to trust kinesiology more than I trust modern pharmaceutical science. Imagine a testing system of guidance that is accurate and incorruptible by personal interests.

Think of this like a nervous system for science. Kinesiology could be used in large split group testing to instantly guide randomized controlled trails before they begin. Performing RCTs indicated by kinesiology would save time and money. RCTs would be like the cardiovascular system carrying out the science, backing up what was already predicted by kinesiology split groups.

The mind–body connection

Hopefully you are able to connect the dots that our thoughts and feeling affect your health. At present modern medicine has no capacity to understand that someone's life situation is the cause of their fibromyalgia or that someone's autoimmune dysfunction is stress or diet related. They look on symptoms as an enemy that needs to eradicated or destroyed, instead of looking on pain as informative, which is a clue to the cause. In many cases they use strong pharmaceutical medication or invasive surgeries before attempting elimination diets, herbal remedies or exercise prescription.

Hopefully you can see that our body is intelligent. Make no mistake, our body is a biological computer run by our subconscious programming that we were born with and for the most part works without conscious input. Our conscious mind is like a person tapping the keyboard to enter commands, but the computer code and programming run the nuts and bolts of the computer. We can observe the body and its healing ability, the inner workings of us, controlled by our innate intelligence that lives inside us, the force of life. We can measure the precise output of life but why life exists may always be a mystery, like the mystery of the stars and the universe.

What is within our control is our mindset, which is our internal response to situations, our filters (how we interpret the world), beliefs systems and awareness. Our mindset has the power to make us sick or the power to heal us rapidly. The power of the mind offers a choice that we control if we are willing to review our current mindset with non-judgement, self-love and forgiveness. Are we victims of circumstances or are we masters of our destiny? Living a principled lifestyle based on a philosophy that makes sense to us will help us master our own destiny.

Learning about the environment and the story of the universe will cast a new perspective on our place in the universe. We are a piece of Earth's many parts; this is the only known habitat suitable for life, not just in our solar system, but in the universe. Being grateful is one way we can show our appreciation of nature's blessings and Earth's long history before we arrived.

Great civilizations came and went before us. History tells us a story of their triumphs but also their falls. We would do well to study these past civilizations so that we might not make the same the mistakes they did and become history along with them.

Killing us softly

In our determination to make our lives more comfortable we are inadvertently shortening our lives and becoming unhealthier than previous generations. Prolonged sitting, poor nutrition due to a diet of junk food, lack of exercise and overexposure to screen time are killing us softly. Our perceived comfort and avoidance of all types of challenges is doing us more harm than good. If we could see the damage this comfort bubble is causing us we would be shocked.

Blunt trauma is immediate and clear of cause, whereas these soft micro-traumas are causing disease slowly and insidiously, and that disease becomes the tip of an iceberg. Someone at any point could prevent a disease by addressing their lifestyle or psychological wellness. Our determination to live in a comfortable bubble, away from challenges or pain, accumulates micro-traumas that will ironically result in an irreversible challenge of chronic pain and disease.

Time is limited by our biological clock. We are a mortal sponge, wrung out to soak up fresh water over and again in a lifetime. When our bodies are living a healthy life we are wringing our sponge, to allow the flow of life through us; however, when we living in the comfort bubble, our cellular water will become stagnant, which is detrimental to our health. The essential commodity in this life is time and organizing a healthy lifestyle balancing challenges and comfort will give us the best chance of living a long healthy and happy life.

As suggested in this book, seek advice from a holistic professional. A practitioner who can treat our physical symptoms as well as heal our emotional issues is the future of healthcare. They will help break the conditioning that pain is an absolute must as we age. Most musculoskeletal pain can be traced back to alignment issues and by removing them this will at least reduce pain. When we experience pain, this is best viewed as informative; we do not need to fear pain, but instead understand it.

Watching TV, excessively using our phones and social media are changing our culture more quickly than at any time in history. Most people would go as far to say they couldn't live without them, but in reality these are relatively new inventions. Before they arrived we did just fine and if they were to disappear tomorrow we would be just fine. Our time is limited and how you use your time is a choice. If you are prioritizing your time on unhealthy pursuits that make you feel good, but yield no long-term benefit, this is a recipe for health issues, mental and physical.

We are amazing creatures in the sense that we are progressively intelligent, creating remarkable technology, the sciences, art, philosophy and spirituality, but in the not too distant past we were animals, more related to a monkey than artificial intelligence. My advice is use technology but don't let technology use you. Begin to question; draw your own conclusions instead of parroting the narrative of others.

Stress positions

When I was at school one of our PE teachers took us to the gym hall and made everyone stand in stress positions for an extended period, which some people would consider barbaric now – a teacher stressing a child until they gave up. When I was in the Marines I did this several times in training. I could have given up at any moment and, trust me, the thought crossed my mind on several occasions.

Sometimes the thrashings as they were known were not fair; one corporal said he was thrashing us because his wife was giving him a hard time and in his anger he was passing this on to us. Mostly this was done with a glint in their eye, dressed up as being serious.

In the Marines this is seen a character building – life isn't fair sometimes. In life or death situations, there is no time to be offended or question authority – the situation requires a cool head and executive decisions to navigate it, until survival is assured and reflection can begin. There is no point reflecting if you are dead.

Therefore stress and pain aren't always detrimental to us and can be a springboard to achieve our ambitions that would otherwise be unattainable. Most of the time we avoid pain, mainly because of fear or self-doubt, but the irony is that fear and self-doubt have the potential to cause more harm to us than avoiding pain at all costs.

Modern stoicism

A patient of mine who has had fantastic results is a remarkable woman. When I first met her she'd been suffering with constant neck pain for some time and she had already had a neck and shoulder operation, which didn't solve the problem. When she started as a patient I was cautious of the results we could achieve because of the operation and the progressive severity of her problem.

She participated in a posture correction program and to my surprise she had far better results than I expected, resolving her neck and shoulder issues. I see her for a periodic maintenance appointment now and she does two Pilates classes a week, which was not achievable in the beginning. She now feels younger than she did when she first came to see me.

Her secret is her mindset. Even though she'd had a neck operation, she was open to making changes, as opposed to many people that wear the badge of honour to say that their pain 'is just old age' or 'it'll never change, that just me'; she was willing to believe in the unreasonable. Decades before seeing me she'd had an emotional trauma due to a tragic accident that left her daughter permanently disabled. Like most people of her era she put this in her blind spot, unable at the time to process this trauma.

Many years later she had this dream where she was holding her organs outside of her body; in a panic she dropped the organs and was is dragging them behind her to seek advice from her father. He gently touched her cheek and gave her some words of reassurance. She then sought advice from her aunt and uncle and they were dancing while smiling at her. Lastly she saw two paramedics and they only broke their conversation to tell her they would be with her in a minute, at which point she woke up.

This dream lay dormant for many years until she had counselling and the significance of the dream was revealed. When the time came she could recall every detail, drawing the conclusion that dragging her organs around represented an acknowledgment she needed to compartmentalize this trauma in order to heal. She was always going grieve the lost but she also needed to move on as her dream archetypes showed her.

To not forget but to compartmentalize them, so that she could move on. Before this insight this unresolved trauma in her blind spot was unconsciously affecting her behaviour, so she was unable to heal her emotional wound. She wrote a poem called 'The Griever's Dream' that won an award and she read this to an audience. (appendix 1 page XXX).

I was in the editing phase of this book when I asked to her if I could use her story and she told me about the poem. When I saw the poem about 'inside out' I knew something magical was happening: the coincidence that I would write a book about developing an inside-out mindset and my patient was telling me about an award-winning poem she wrote about her insides being outside. I had already written my poem at the front about the fatality and inevitability of our declining health and I decided to name this poem 'The Living Dream', a play on 'The Griever's Dream'.

Her dad was Second World War veteran. The greatest generations were also the most silent. She told me when he and his friends returned from the war, they never spoke about their time on the battlefield. They put these events into a blind spot, determined to rebuild their lives; that was their generation's way. She said they went to Arnhem only a few years ago to the site of Operation Market Garden and her dad opened up about his experiences, which he'd never spoken about with her before. He and most of his generation were strong, hard people that could hold in their experiences because they didn't want to burden others.

My patient processed her trauma, exercising modern stoicism. We don't need to be as hard as the greatest generation or make the sacrifices they collectively did so that we can live in freedom today. They put their problems into a blind spot so that they could be brave, and in some cases fight to the death to protect our liberties. Modern stoicism is acknowledging our feelings, without becoming a victim, remaining pragmatic, solution focused and maintaining tolerance of others, exercising forgiveness of the past in the same way the greatest generation magnanimously did after the world wars.

And lastly

No religion, race or gender is responsible for the past. The past has no right or wrong, the past just is. We cannot collectively progress on the path of raising consciousness if we seek revenge and retribution retrospectively; instead we must exercise forgiveness and understanding. We cannot learn from people of the past if we judge them by the present. They were people of their time and we must be people of ours. It is our responsibility to the people of tomorrow that we show compassion and tolerance, so that they may do the same.

We must rise above the **FEAR** to show our descendants they do not need to be afraid, that they are part of a family of the world and we stick together. I will finish with the sage advice of Ian Brown's acronym of fear:

Forgive Everybody And Remember,
For Everything A Reason.

Appendix

The Griever's Dream

Knees bent I strain, then looking down see glistening pink,
My liver and my pulsing heart.
Extending arms I scoop the overflowing steaming mass.
'Must not let go.'
My insides, outside, beat and slide away from me.
'Must hold on.'
My mouth framing into gaping O, I howl,
'Help me.'
But who can help to bear the strain of so much weight ?
Fascinating, but terrifying I sees the rhythm of my insides,
    outside.
'I recognize them for they are me.'
Gingerly I rise and grasp them with aching arms.
Who would have thought such weight of insides when outside?
I move away and cry,
'Help me.'
Familiar face lovingly speak , 'You are my sweet,' but no help.
I move with stealthy step,
'Hold on don't let them slip.'
These precious parts so pale and pure.
A kidney, gyrating guts, moving to the ground.
'Must not let go.'
Such quantity and beauty of my insides outside.
'Help me.'
Strangers dance and smile, no time for help.
Classical columns call, 'Here rest on us.'
I rest, but too heavy are my insides, outside.
I see my grief and rage exposed and raw,
As familiar as old friends. 'Must I always wear my insides,
    outside?'
'Yes,' they whisper back, 'For we are you, inside or outside.'
    – Susannah Griffin

Book Available

If you've enjoyed this book why don't you check out this book?

Find this book on Amazon:
The Back Doctor Secrets: Take back control of your health... physically, mentally, emotionally and spiritually. Secrets We Used To Know.

The Back Doctor
Chiropractic

About the Author

David Tennison has been a successful personal trainer, exercise referral specialist for GPs and a chiropractor. With the knowledge and skill that he has honed and developed over the years, he now likens himself to a concept he devised called the Hybrid Practitioner, which more accurately describes him and his treatment.

He believes the Hybrid Practitioner can focus on isolated symptoms but is always thinking holistically to the symptoms' cause, making them part physician and part psychologist. He also believes teaching people about their health is a solution to the world's health problems. He has written one other book called *The Back Doctor Secrets*.

Acknowledgments

Notable mentions are my friend and business coach Tim Rylatt, who wrote a foreword for this book and is a former police officer. Thanks Anya Wanguwan for all illustrations and diagrams contained in the book and Nikki Goodeve for cover photography. Thank you Andrew Chapman for editing and typesetting and Rob Wheele for the cover design.

A thank you to my sister Helen Tennison (soon to be Baxter) for reading my first book, to prove someone did! She works within the NHS and she kindly offered to read through a draft of this book before going to print. Susannah Griffin for kindly letting me use her poem in the appendix and her dad's story in my conclusion. Other kind readers before print were Patrick Hogg, Di Laker, Noah Strut, Michael Ralls, Julia King, Alberto Giovino, Carol Baxter, Julia King and Penny King (no relation, just synchronicity at work).

Lastly to my patients that heal me as much as I heal them.